Joy to the World

Advent-Christmas Meditations with St. Francis de Sales

Rev. Dr. Santhiyagu Arockiyasamy, msfs

LEONINE PUBLISHERS
PHOENIX, ARIZONA

Printed With Ecclesiastical Permission. ✠ Most Reverend Earl Boyea. September 12, 2014.

Published by Leonine Publishers LLC
Phoenix, Arizona
USA

ISBN-13: 978-1-942190-04-2

10 9 8 7 6 5 4 3 2 1

Printed in the United States of America

Visit us online at www.leoninepublishers.com
For more information: info@leoninepublishers.com

Acknowledgments

It has been said that "at times our own light goes out and is rekindled by a spark from another person. Each of us has a cause to think with deep gratitude of those who have lighted the flame within us" (Albert Schweitzer). I am here with a grateful heart to appreciate many people who have inspired and encouraged me to complete this work. At the outset, I would like to thank the Most Rev. Earl Boyea, Bishop of the Diocese of Lansing, Michigan, for his fraternal encouragement, and the Most Rev. Carl F. Mengeling, Bishop Emeritus, for blessing my humble efforts with his message. I owe my gratitude to the Most Rev. Steven J. Raica, Bishop of the Diocese of Gaylord, Michigan; Msgr. Michael D. Murphy; and Msgr. Robert D. Lunsford, for their friendship, appreciation, and valuable suggestions. I would also like to express my sincere thanks to Rev. Dr. Abraham Vettuvelil, msfs, our Superior General; Rev. Anthony Dharma Raj, msfs, the Provincial of the South-East (India) Province of the Fransalians; and Rev. Augustine Tharappel, msfs, the Vice-Provincial of the USA Vice Province, for their fraternal love and guidance.

I owe my gratitude also to all my Fransalian and other priest friends for their timely help and loving support, and in a special way to my Fransalian brother priests in our Michigan Fransalian community, for they walked with me and showed me their love and support. They have been so gracious and kind in their appreciation and in encouraging me to complete this work. I also gratefully remember and thank my friends, especially the staff and the people of St. Mary's Parish in Flint, Michigan, for their help and encouragement in writing this book. I gratefully appreciate the effort of Mr. Joe Darnell in designing the cover page. As many people have become instruments of God's blessings in my life, I am glad that I have become a little instrument to bring this book into your hands. I hope that it will inspire you during this holy season to find Jesus in your life and to experience His love.

In love and gratitude,

Rev. Dr. Santhiyagu Arockiyasamy, msfs

Dedication

To Rev. A. Louis and Rev. Sisters of the
Salesian Missionaries of Mary Immaculate
(SMMI), Tamil Nadu, India, who inspired
And motivated me to listen to God's call and
Persevere in my religious vocation to the priesthood

Contents

Foreword

The season of Advent has been given penitential, eschatological, and joyful flavors over the years. Often this led to disagreements about what exactly should occur during these weeks before Christmas. Fr. Santhiyagu Arockiyasamy wishes us to focus on *Joy* as an interpretive key, not only to Advent but to the Holy Season of Christmas as well.

These meditations are based on scriptural texts and, as he calls it, the "wisdom" of St. Francis de Sales. This saint has been a tremendous blessing to the Church for his ability to translate spirituality into very concrete and practical advice. My prayer is that, during this Advent and Christmas, those who use this book will find moments of real grace in the ordinary events of our days. These will then only increase our joy and make it complete.

✠ Most Rev. Earl Boyea
Bishop of Lansing, Michigan
Advent 2014

Introduction

Pope Francis, in his Christmas homily of 2013, said, "On this night let us share the joy of the Gospel: God loves us, He so loves us that He has given us His Son to be our brother, to be light in our darkness. As the angels said to the shepherds: 'Do not be afraid,' the Lord repeats to us, 'Do not be afraid!' (Lk 2:10). And I also repeat to all of you: Do not be afraid! Our Father loves us, always forgives and gives us Jesus to guide us on the way. Jesus is the light who brightens the darkness." The Advent Season announces this Good News: that God is visiting us to make us a people of hope and joy. The incarnation of Jesus assures us that God is in our midst and the world is filled with boundless joy because of our loving God.

We must know that "joy is the true gift of Christmas, not the expensive gifts that call for time and money. We can communicate this joy simply with a smile, a kind gesture, a little help, and acts of forgiveness. And the joy we give will certainly come back to us. Let us pray that this presence of the liberating joy of God shines forth in our lives" (Pope Benedict XVI). Christmas is all about experiencing the joy of the Lord's birth and becoming a channel of joy to our world. This little book contains wisdom from the Gospel Message of Jesus and the spiritual teachings of St. Francis de Sales. Its purpose is to encourage, motivate and enlighten its readers to understand the true meaning of this holy season, to grow in faith and find Jesus in their lives. If you realize that Jesus asks you to spend just five to ten minutes of your time with Him at any hour of the day, then surely this book can be of good help in motivating you to listen to God's word, to meditate peacefully, and pray confidently. I wish you God's blessings on your efforts to grow in Christian perfection in this holy season and become a people of joy and peace.

Rev. Dr. Santhiyagu Arockiyasamy, msfs
Flint, Michigan

Advent Season - Waiting in Hope

"Jesus has entered our history; he has shared our journey.
He came to free us from darkness and to grant us light.
In him was revealed the grace, the mercy,
And the tender love of the Father…"
(Pope Francis)

First Week - Hope

"Since you want to belong entirely to God,
Why be afraid of your weakness on which in
Any case you shouldn't be relying; you do hope
In God, don't you? And will anyone who hopes
In Him ever be put to shame? No, never."
(St. Francis de Sales)

Monday of the First Week of Advent

Is 4:2–6 (I); Is 2:1–5 (II); Mt 8:5–11

Preparation: Take a few minutes of silence, setting aside all your worries and anxieties, and become aware of the divine presence.

Listening to God's Word: "When Jesus heard this, he was amazed and said to those following him, 'Amen, I tell you, in no one in Israel have I found such faith. I say to you, many will come from the east and the west, and will recline with Abraham, Isaac, and Jacob at the banquet in the kingdom of heaven'" (Mt 8:10–11).

The Messiah's coming

The people of Israel had been waiting longingly for God's powerful intervention, through the coming of a Messiah who, they hoped, would restore their glorious days of political power and prosperity. The prophets prepared the people for that great day, calling them to repentance and renewal. Today's Gospel announces the outcome of the Messiah's coming: the creation of a new people of God. In the Gospel narrative there are two images relevant for our reflection: the healing of the servant by Jesus (Mt 8:5–13) and the proclamation that "many will come from the east and the west" (8:11) to dine at the salvation banquet of the Lord. These two events are images that signify the messianic fulfillment. The physical healing foretells restoration for people who are broken physically and spiritually. Jesus, as a Jewish teacher who extended the blessings of God's reign to a pagan leader of the occupying Roman army, would have caused scandal. Yet, by the unconditional faith of the Centurion, Jesus healed his servant. In this context, Jesus also uses the image of the gathering of people "from the east and the west" to dine in God's kingdom. This referred to the reunion of the Jews, who were scattered in exile, with God's people in Jerusalem (cf. Is 43:5; Bar 4:37). However, by bringing the blessings of salvation to the Centurion's home, Jesus used this image to signify the restoration of people divided and dispersed on many grounds. With the birth of Jesus the Messiah, the gathering of the dispersed children of God into one people (cf. Jn 11:52) has begun, transcending all the barriers and dividing walls.

As a people of faith earnestly desiring to share God's gift of salvation, we must repent and believe in Jesus just like the Centurion. Isaiah speaks about the glorious days of Zion in the messianic age that were marked by peace, joy, and the absence of violence. He used the symbols of plow shares and pruning hooks, which are tools of cultivation and transformation; swords and spears are tools of war and violence (cf. Is 2:4). The prophet urges us to change these symbols of war and violence (which represent hatred, selfishness, injustice, enmity and death) into symbols of plowshares and pruning hooks (which are signs of love, compassion, truth, justice and fraternal solidarity). This is the consequence of the Messiah's birth in our midst. Pope Paul VI said that "we consider Christmas as the encounter, the greatest encounter, the historical encounter, the decisive encounter between God and mankind. He who has faith knows this truly; let him rejoice." As we prepare to encounter Jesus during this Advent season, let us realize that we are called to transcend all our differences among us and gather around Him as one community of believers. Ask yourself: how am I prepared to welcome the Messiah into my life? Do I overcome the barriers and the dividing walls to welcome others and walk with them in love? What efforts will I make this Advent to avoid inflicting spiritual and emotional injury on others?

Wisdom from St. Francis de Sales: "Oh, how happy we would be to have alive in us all that our titles signify! For instance, it is not enough to call ourselves priest, bishop, or religious. Our actual lives must be congruent with these titles. We must take care of the charge we exercise and of the vocation in which we live. In short, we must assess how well our passions and affections are controlled, and whether our actions are congruent with our state of life" (Nuns of the Visitation (trans.), *The Sermons of St. Francis de Sales for Advent and Christmas,* 100-101).

Prayer: Lord Jesus, thank You for becoming one of us through Your Incarnation. Help me to forgive injuries and grudges, so that I will overcome the barriers which separate me from others.

Tuesday of the First Week of Advent

Is 11:1–10; Lk 10:21–24

Preparation: Take a few minutes of silence, setting aside all your worries and anxieties, and become aware of the divine presence.

Listening to God's Word: "At that very moment he rejoiced (in) the holy Spirit and said, 'I give you praise, Father, Lord of heaven and earth, for although you have hidden these things from the wise and the learned you have revealed them to the childlike'" (Lk 10:21).

A prayer of praise

When the disciples asked the Master how one can experience God's goodness in life, the spiritual Master said, "We can experience God's goodness and love if we learn to be grateful in the best and faithful in the worst." As today's Gospel presents, Jesus, experiencing God as a loving Father, recognized the Father's revelation in the simple and ordinary events of human life and in the little people. The context of Jesus' prayer of praise was the disciples' success in proclaiming the Gospel to different towns and villages. Empowered by the Holy Spirit, they drove out evil spirits and healed the sick. Encouraged by the disciples' success, Jesus praised and thanked the Father for such a profound revelation through the disciples (cf. Lk 10:21). Thomas Merton said, "Advent reminds us that 'the last things' are already present and realized in a hidden manner. God's kingdom is already 'in our midst.' But, the mystery can only be known by those who in faith enter into it, who find their place in the mystical Christ, and therefore find the mystery of Christ realized and fulfilled in themselves." Honest awareness and recognition of God's presence, by accepting life's realities, will prompt us to follow God's will and enter into a personal relationship with God and with one another.

At the time of Jesus' earthly life, the scribes and the religious leaders were regarded as the clever and the wise. The poor, the uneducated, and the children were among those belonging to "the accursed people" of the country because they did not know anything about the law, had no education, and did not make an effort to avoid sin in their lives. That was the reason that a scribe could say, "An uneducated person is not a virtuous person." The disciples of Jesus were uneducated, simple, and ordinary persons in the society of their time, yet God chose them and manifested His power through them. Therefore, Jesus rejoiced in the Spirit, praising and thanking the Father for such a revelation. It is God's personal union with humanity that enables us to experience the dearness of God as a loving Father. By this divine relationship, shared with us through Jesus' Incarnation (cf. Jn 1:14), a perfect harmony is created in our world, where enmity and animosities are dissolved; where the wolf and lamb, calf and lion, cow and bear, live in harmony (cf. Is 11:6–9). Thus, the whole creation is healed, renewed and restored to wholeness. We must come before God with simplicity and openness of heart to become channels of God's messianic blessings in our world. As Blessed Teresa of Calcutta said, "It is Christmas every time you let God love others through you...yes, it is Christmas every time you smile at your brothers/sisters and offer him/her your hand in loving service." Ask yourself: during this Advent season, do I cultivate the attitude of praise and thanksgiving for God's many blessings, which I receive each day through Jesus? Am I ready to find God's hand guiding me in the ordinariness of life? In what ways do I allow Jesus to love others through me?

Wisdom from St. Francis de Sales: "We ought most certainly to repeat it [the name of Jesus] often during our lifetime, for it was given to His Son by the Eternal Father. It is a name which is above every other name, wholly divine, gentle and full of goodness. It is an oil poured out (Cant 1:2) to heal all the wounds of our souls. It is the name which gives joy to the angels, saves men and women, and causes demons to tremble. This is why it should be deeply engraved upon our hearts and our spirits so that, blessing it and honoring it in this life, we may be worthy of singing with the blessed: Live Jesus! Live Jesus!" (Visitation, *The Sermons of SFS for Advent and Christmas,* 101-102).

Prayer: God our Father, thank You for revealing Your goodness in my human littleness and sinfulness. In Your mercy, lift me up when I fall, that I may become a person of praise and gratitude.

Wednesday of the First Week of Advent

Is 25:6–10a; Mt 15:29–37

Preparation: Take a few minutes of silence, setting aside all your worries and anxieties, and become aware of the divine presence.

Listening to God's Word: "Great crowds came to him having with them the lame, the blind, the deformed, the mute, and many others. They placed them at his feet, and he cured them. Jesus summoned his disciples and said, 'My heart is moved with pity for the crowd, for they have been with me now for three days and have nothing to eat'" (Mt 15:30, 32).

The great crowds

Once, a disciple asked the Master, "What shall I do to love my neighbor?" "Stop hating yourself." The disciple pondered these words for a long time and came back to say, "But I love myself too much, for I am selfish and self-centered. How do I get rid of that?" "Be friendly to yourself and your self will be contented and it will set you free to love your neighbor" (Anthony de Mello, *One Minute Wisdom*, 131). To experience and express genuine love, we must come out of ourselves and reach out to others in love. The season of Advent is a season of joy and hope, which invites us to grow in that love. C. S. Lewis says that "just as every natural event is the manifestation at a particular place and moment of nature's total character, so every particular Christian miracle manifests at a particular place and moment the significance of the Incarnation." Jesus, the Messiah, acted with compassion, spoke hope-giving words, and brought healing and comfort to those who were afflicted and broken-hearted. The great crowds that followed him were made up of afflicted, wounded and despised people. We should notice that the crowd of people in the Gospel narrative came to Jesus broken, sick and suffering; and they went back home healed, strengthened, and restored to wholeness of health (cf. Mt 15:30–32). By healing their physical illnesses, offering them spiritual comfort, and feeding them in their hunger, Jesus fulfilled the messianic prophecies foretold by the prophet Isaiah.

The prophet proclaimed that at the coming of the Messiah the eyes of the blind would be opened, the ears of the deaf would be unstopped, the lame would leap like a deer, and the tongue of the speechless would sing for joy (cf. Is 35:5–6, 29:18–19). This reminds us that the God of Israel is a compassionate God who will wipe away the tears from all faces, and the disgrace of his people he will take away from all the earth (cf. Is 25:8). This messianic prophecy was fulfilled in Jesus who relieved people from the bondage of pain and suffering. The great crowd of people in the Gospel narrative resembles the great crowd of our world. The majority of the people in the world today are afflicted by various illnesses, are manipulated and subjugated, and suffer hunger and poverty and many other evils. There are many among us who long for love and affection, for comfort and compassion. Jesus calls each one of us to continue His saving work. We must recognize the great crowd of people around us and listen to their cry. Most often such people become the missing voices in our world. We must identify and help them to experience God's saving grace by our words of encouragement and appreciation, and by our acts of kindness and love. Ask yourself: do I recognize and listen to the cries of the wounded people around me? How do I offer them the message of hope to alleviate their pain and suffering?

Wisdom from St. Francis de Sales: "There are two reasons why people do not profit by the word of God. The first is the procrastination. People postpone the accomplishment of God's word until tomorrow. Alas! We poor creatures do not realize that our good is found in the present moment, which is today. Our life is the today in which we are living, in this present moment in which we are living and enjoying. The second reason is 'spiritual avarice' by which we seek to obtain a great deal of knowledge and to amass a huge stock of devotional exercises. Live each day well and you will nourish yourself well by putting God's word into practice. Leave the rest to Divine Providence, which will surely provide sufficiently for your needs" (Visitation, *The Sermons of SFS for Advent and Christmas*, 38-39).

Prayer: Lord Jesus, thank You for Your steadfast love and forgiveness. Help me to avoid prejudice and to show love and compassion to the poor and suffering people around me.

Thursday of the First Week of Advent

Is 26:1–6; Mt 7:21, 24–27

Preparation: Take a few minutes of silence, setting aside all your worries and anxieties, and become aware of the divine presence.

Listening to God's Word: "Not everyone who says to me 'Lord, Lord,' will enter the kingdom of heaven, but only the one who does the will of my Father in heaven. Everyone who listens to these words of mine and acts on them will be like a wise man who built his house on rock" (Mt 7:21, 24).

Discipleship is not in words alone

Once, in a village there was a woman who was deeply religious and filled with love for God. Every day she attended Mass, and had never missed it in her whole life. Each morning on her way back from the church, children used to call out to her; poor people asked for a little help, and others used to greet her. She was so immersed in her devotions that she did not even notice any of them. One day she went to church just in time for the service. She pushed the door of the church, but it didn't open. She pushed it harder, but found that the door was locked. Distressed and upset that she would be missing Mass for the first time in her life, and not knowing what to do, she looked up. There, right in front of her eyes, was a note on the door that read, "I am out there." Therefore, it is said that "the important religious distinction is not between those who worship and those who do not worship but between those who love and those who don't love" (cf. De Mello, *Prayer of the Frog,* 70). Following Jesus does not mean just keeping some rules and regulations, saying some prayers, observing certain rituals, and speaking eloquently about God. Rather, it demands that we live by love as Jesus has taught us. Since the Beatitudes are the guiding principles for believers, Jesus concluded this great teaching by telling us that we must not only listen to but actually act upon His words. This involves not merely obeying Him in words alone but in concrete acts of love and goodness, because it is not those who say 'Lord, Lord,' who will enter the kingdom of heaven but only those who listen to His words and live by them (Mt 7:21). The Divine Word that we read and reflect upon must touch our hearts and affect the way in which we live our daily lives.

As followers of Jesus, we cannot be passive hearers of God's word; we must be active doers. To accomplish this, we must have a discerning mind and a loving heart. We must come before the Lord with our hearts open to welcome Him and accept in trust all that He will send us; we must listen to Him speaking to us, whether through others or through life's events. We should learn to discern God's will in everything that happens to us and make the right decisions in total submission to God's purpose for us. As persons of loving hearts, following the example of Jesus, we must be ready to listen to Jesus speaking to us in the missing voices of people around us. Moved by our faith conviction, we will be prompted to act like Jesus our Master, diffusing love and compassion to everyone, and thereby proving our identity as disciples of Jesus. We will neither be shaken nor will we fall because we are grounded on Jesus, our rock. Saint Augustine said that God's best servant is the one who does not expect always to hear the answer he or she desires, but who always ends up desiring whatever he or she hears from God. If we follow the Lord in faithfulness we will neither stumble nor struggle because the Lord is our only security (cf. Is 26:1–5). Our lives must announce the purpose of Jesus' Incarnation: that He came to illuminate the world by His wisdom and fill it with His love. Ask yourself: do I listen to God's Word with an open heart, and live by It so as to find happiness and meaning in life? Have I learned to say "yes" to God in everything, and to face life with optimism and courage?

Wisdom from St. Francis de Sales: "Everyone is obliged to strive for the perfection of Christian life, because our Lord commands that we be perfect (Mt 5:48) and St. Paul says the same (2 Cor 13:11). Perfection of Christian life consists in conforming our will to that of our good God, who is the sovereign standard and norm for all actions. So in order to acquire perfection we must always consider and recognize what God's will is in everything that concerns us, so that we can flee what He wants us to avoid and accomplish what He wants us to do" (Jeane Peronne Marie Thibert, *Letters of Spiritual Direction,* 105).

Prayer: Loving Jesus, thank You for calling me to be Your disciple. Motivate me with Your Spirit to follow You not only in words, but by living a daily life of faithfulness and loving kindness.

Friday of the First Week of Advent

Is 29:17–24; Mt 9:27–31

Preparation: Take a few minutes of silence, setting aside all your worries and anxieties, and become aware of the divine presence.

Listening to God's Word: "And as Jesus passed on from there, two blind men followed (him), crying out, 'Son of David, have pity on us!' ...Jesus said to them, 'Do you believe that I can do this?' 'Yes, Lord,' they said to him. Then he touched their eyes and said, 'Let it be done for you according to your faith'" (Mt 9:27–29).

Seeking God's goodness

In the midst of the hum-drum routine of life and our daily anxieties, the Liturgy of the Word brings us the message that God loves us despite our weaknesses, sinfulness, frailties and failures; that through Him, we become worthy of His goodness and mercy. The disciple kept asking each day, "How shall I find God?" And each time the Master gave the same answer: "Through desire." "But I desire God with all my heart and soul, don't I? Then why have I not found Him?" the disciple insisted. Days passed. One day the Master was bathing in the river with the disciple. Suddenly he pushed the disciple headlong underwater and held him there until the poor fellow struggled to breathe air. Immediately bringing the disciple out of the water, the Master asked him, "Why did you struggle while you were under water?" "Because I was gasping for air." Now the Master said, "If your desire is so intense in seeking God as you desired to gasp for air, you will find God." This is what happened to the two blind men who took a leap of faith in their desire for God's mercy, breaking from their past experience of humiliation and abandonment. Believing and trusting in the power of Jesus to change the condition of their lives, they earnestly prayed for his mercy, crying out, "Have mercy on us, O Son of David." It is a very simple, but powerful, prayer of trust.

These two men had experienced abandonment and rejection by everyone in society. Yet they longingly desired for God's goodness, and consequently their faith-filled prayer moved Jesus to heal them. They experienced God's goodness in Jesus and proclaimed it wherever they went. Isaiah proclaimed that "On that day the deaf shall hear the words of a book; And out of gloom and darkness, the eyes of the blind shall see. The lowly will ever find joy in the Lord, and the poor rejoice in the Holy One of Israel" (Is 29:18–19). This is the result of God's love and mercy for His impoverished people. The two blind men earnestly longed and prayed for such messianic blessings and experienced them through Jesus. We too must seek the goodness and mercy of God without giving up. Henri Nouwen said that "we are whom God made us to be in his infinite love. We are the gifts we are given, not just the conquests we make. As long as we keep running around, anxiously trying to affirm ourselves or be affirmed by others, we remain blind to One who has loved us first, dwells in our heart and has formed our truest self" (from James E. Adams, *Living Hope*, 9). We must pray for the Lord's mercy as did those blind men; we must pray for healing, not only from physical blindness but also from our spiritual blindness: our unfaithfulness, our prejudice and our self-justifying attitudes. Therefore, ask yourself pondering the teachings of Jesus: do I let my ears and heart be open to hear the cry of the poor and the suffering? What initiative do I take in bringing God's goodness and mercy to people around me, in order to create a better world?

Wisdom from St. Francis de Sales: "Though everything turns and changes about us, we must always remain firm, our eyes fixed on God seeking Him and moving towards Him. A ship may sail in different directions, north or south, east or west driven by various winds, yet the needle of its compass will always point toward the pole star. Whether we are in sadness or joy, in consolation or bitterness, in peace or trouble, light or darkness, in temptation or tranquility, in liking or disgust, in dryness or warmth, scorched by the sun or refreshed by the dew, yet the highest point of our heart, of our spirit, of our superior will, which is the needle of our compass must always be turned to God our creator and Savior" (SFS, *Introduction to the Devout Life (IDL), Part IV,* Ch. 13, 319).

Prayer: Jesus my Savior, thank You for seeking after me, to heal and save me. Help me to find You in my life's events and experiences, that I might always long for Your goodness and mercy.

Saturday of the First Week of Advent

Is 30:19–21, 23–26; Mt 9:35–10:1, 5a, 6–8

Preparation: Take a few minutes of silence, setting aside all your worries and anxieties, and become aware of the divine presence.

Listening to God's Word: "Jesus went around to all the towns and villages, teaching in their synagogues, proclaiming the gospel of the kingdom, and curing every disease and illness. At the sight of the crowds, his heart was moved with pity for them because they were troubled and abandoned, like sheep without a shepherd" (Mt 9:35–36).

God of Compassion

When we are in great trouble, or going through pain and suffering, we long for immediate relief, support and healing. We intensely desire that God do something miraculous to deliver us from our trials. Today's Liturgy of the Word presents Jesus, Who is moved by compassion to free people from their distress and suffering. Once, a man was lost in a desert. Later, when describing his ordeal to his friends, he told how, in sheer despair, he had knelt down in that lonely place and cried out to God for help. "And did God answer your prayer?" one of his friends asked him. "Oh, no! Before God could come to my aid, an explorer appeared and showed me the way" (De Mello, *Prayer of the Frog*, 136). Often God's compassion and blessings come to us in disguise. We conveniently pass them by without recognizing or appreciating them. The people of Israel were told by prophets such as Isaiah about the coming Messiah and His saving works (cf. Is 30:19, 26). Now they could witness and experience that prophecy in reality, coming to fulfillment in Jesus. The images of harassed, helpless sheep-without-a-shepherd signify most people's life experience of hardship and misery. Jesus' compassionate actions show God's deep love for all such people.

Isaiah says, "O people of Zion, who dwell in Jerusalem, no more will you weep; He will be gracious to you when you cry out, as soon as he hears he will answer you" (Is 30:19). Such an assurance of God's Divine protection has been actualized in Jesus, Who in turn commissioned the disciples to continue His saving work (cf. Mt 10:6–8). This shows us that

God's saving work is not finished once and for all with Jesus' earthly life. The Lord continues to intervene in the lives of people and to hear their cry. Therefore, every one of us has the obligation to bring the Good News of the Lord's compassion to the world, through concrete actions of loving kindness. Jesus said, "Without cost you have received; without cost you are to give" (Mt 10:8). Our little acts of goodness, however simple, can manifest the Lord's compassion. As Henry Nouwen said, "We keep praying to the almighty and powerful God. But God's power is something entirely different. God does not want us to be afraid, distant or envious. God wants to come close, very close, so close that we can rest in the intimacy of God as children in their mother's arms" (James E. Adams, *Living Hope*, 7). Through His acts of healing and His compassion for the sick, the suffering and the neglected, Jesus revealed God as compassionate and merciful. Pope Francis prays: "May we not be robbed of hope, because this strength is a grace, a gift from God which carries us forward with our eyes fixed on heaven." Ask yourself: do I believe that the Lord is gracious and merciful, slow to anger and abounding in love and goodness? How do I regard those who are suffering and struggling in life: with compassion or condemnation?

Wisdom from St. Francis de Sales: "The means to unite yourself with the neighbor are these: we must regard our neighbor in God, who wills that we should love and cherish him. We must exercise ourselves in this love of our neighbor, expressing it externally. And although it may seem at first against our will, we must not give up on that account; our repugnance will at last be conquered by habit and good inclination, which will be produced by repetition of the acts. After having prayed to love God, we must always pray to love our neighbor, and especially those to whom our will is not attracted. I advise you to take care sometimes to visit hospitals, comfort the sick, be compassionate to those in infirmities, and pray for them, at the same time giving them some help" (SFS, *Thy Will Be Done,* 45-46).

Prayer: Lord Jesus, thank You for revealing to me the Father's love and compassion. Help me to be kind and compassionate, that others may experience Your love through me.

Second Week - Peace

"In all things and everywhere we must live peacefully;
If troubles either interior or exterior come upon us,
We should receive them peacefully."
(St. Francis de Sales)

Monday of the Second Week of Advent

Is 35:1–10; Lk 5:17–26

Preparation: Take a few minutes of silence, setting aside all your worries and anxieties, and become aware of the divine presence.

Listening to God's Word: "And some men brought on a stretcher a man who was paralyzed; they were trying to bring him in and set (him) in his presence…When he saw their faith, he said, 'As for you, your sins are forgiven…I say to you, rise, pick up your stretcher, and go home'" (Lk 5:18, 20, 24b).

In solidarity with the suffering

The spiritual Master kept insisting to his disciples, "Even if you do great things for others and do not have love, everything is in vain. You keep your good works but must abandon the 'I' and then service would automatically follow. You need not burn your body but burn your ego and naturally love will follow." A little phrase that captures the Gospel message today is "seeing their faith." Jesus had forgiven and healed the paralyzed man because He was moved by the faith of the men who had brought him. This shows the loving solidarity of the community with the suffering member, and Jesus' action of forgiving and healing shows how He found solidarity with those who are sick and suffering. The community took up the responsibility to do something for the individual member in danger. So they brought him to Jesus (cf. Lk 5:18–20). They must have expected only physical healing for the paralyzed man. To their amazement, Jesus bestowed spiritual healing as well. According to Jewish belief at that time, physical infirmities were considered to be a punishment from God for sins committed. Therefore a physical cure depended on the remission of one's sins and guilt. Since sin is an offense against God, it is God alone who has the power to forgive sins.

In this light, Jesus first forgives the man's sins, saying, "Your sins are forgiven" (v. 20). The author of the first letter to Timothy says, "Christ Jesus came into the world to save sinners" (1 Tim 1:15). This is how Jesus the Messiah, in loving solidarity, showed compassion for the sinners and the suffering as He came to seek out and save what was lost (cf. Lk 5:32). Pope Francis says, "God, who is our Father, has sent Jesus to make Himself closer to each one of us, to save us and to forgive all of us, for He always forgives and pardons because He is good and merciful." Our love and concern for others should transcend all our differences, in order to find fraternal solidarity with the suffering members in the community, and to reflect Jesus' love for us. Let us encourage one another to believe in God's promise through the words of Isaiah: "Be strong, fear not! Here is your God, he comes with vindication; ...Then will the eyes of the blind be opened, the ears of the deaf be cleared; Then will the lame leap like a stag, then the tongue of the dumb will sing" (Is 35:4–6). These are concrete actions revealing God's compassionate love for humanity through Jesus. During this Advent and all through our life, we must become agents of such a comforting and hope-giving message for others. As it is said, "Christmas is not a time nor a season, but a state of mind. To cherish peace and goodwill, to be plenteous in mercy, is to have the real spirit of Christmas." Through our attitudes and actions of fraternal solidarity, let us convey the message of compassion to our suffering and afflicted brothers and sisters, so that we are able to bring the true spirit of Christmas back into our Christmas celebrations. Ask yourself: do I create an unfriendly environment around me by my uncaring attitudes? How do I show fraternal solidarity with those facing troubles and difficult moments in life?

Wisdom from St. Francis de Sales: "Theotimus, see that glass of water or that little piece of bread which a holy person gives to one who is poor for God's sake. It is a trivial matter, hardly worth a thought according to human judgment. Yet the Lord rewards it. He immediately repays it with some increase of charity [Mk 9:41]. So the little deeds that flow from charity please God and find a place among meritorious actions. They are in good odor before God's Majesty, and in consideration of them He increases charity" (SFS, *Treatise on the Love of God,* Vol. 1, Book III, Ch. 2, 164).

Prayer: Most Gracious God, thank You for the gift of family and friends. Grant me Your grace, so that I might find fraternal solidarity with others by loving and encouraging them.

Tuesday of the Second Week of Advent

Is 40:1–11; Mt 18:12–14

Preparation: Take a few minutes of silence, setting aside all your worries and anxieties, and become aware of the divine presence.

Listening to God's Word: "What is your opinion? If a man has a hundred sheep and one of them goes astray, will he not leave the ninety-nine in the hills and go in search of the stray? In just the same way, it is not the will of your heavenly Father that one of these little ones be lost" (Mt 18:12, 14).

The importance of the little ones

A father had two sons, and the oldest son was a man of good behavior, and the pride of the family. The youngest son was a person of bad behavior and a disgrace. However, the father was more concerned about his second son and loved him very dearly, so that he went out of his way to help him in his misery. Someone asked him, "Why should you take so much pain to go the extra mile and show personal interest in your disgraceful son rather than being satisfied with your successful son?" The father replied, "The wounded parts of my body need more attention than the rest. So also my strayed son needs my love more than the good one who is safe." The Gospel parable today is concerned with the nature of Christian life in the believing community. The members are to adopt a compassionate and forgiving attitude toward those who go astray. The Gospel parable about the shepherd and the strayed sheep is taken from everyday life, and Jesus used it to teach us a lesson about God's special love for the little ones and the despised. By focusing on the shepherd's decision to leave the ninety-nine and go after the strayed sheep, we are shown the importance of the members who go astray by making mistakes. The author of the first letter to Timothy reminds us that God wants all of us to be saved, so He forgets none but cares for all (1 Tim 2:4). No one can escape the Lord's saving love and compassion. Jesus demonstrated in His life such an unconditional and uncompromising love of God for humanity.

Whether a believer goes astray because of his or her carelessness and negligence, or by the scandal caused by others, none of them should be neglected, because everyone—especially the sinful ones and the little ones—are important, and they need to be loved and cared for. Isaiah speaks of God as "a shepherd [who] feeds his flock; in his arms he gathers the lambs, carrying them in his bosom, and leading the ewes with care" (Is 40:11). For this reason, Jesus, our Savior, became one of us, having been born among the poor and the despised. The Lord says, "You are precious in my eyes and glorious, and I love you. Fear not, for I am with you" (cf. Is 43:4). God values all of us as important and precious despite our failures. Henry Nouwen says that "Christian community is the place where we keep the flame of hope alive among us so that it can grow and become stronger in us. In this way, we can live with courage, trusting that there is a spiritual power in us when we are together that allows us to live in this world without surrendering to the powerful forces constantly seducing us toward despair. That is how we dare to say that God is a God of love when we see hatred all around" (from James E. Adams, *Living Hope*, 11). During this holy season, let us think about this: "Christmas gift suggestions: To your enemy, forgiveness. To an opponent, tolerance. To a friend, your heart. To a customer, service. To all, charity. To every child, a good example. To yourself, respect and honor" (Oren Arnold). Ask yourself: do I value others and appreciate them despite their shortcomings? What are my Christmas-gift options this year?

Wisdom from St. Francis de Sales: "I beg you never to speak evil of your neighbor or say anything, however little, which could offend him. Nevertheless, one must not approve of the evil, flatter it, or try to cover it up, but—when the welfare of the one of whom one speaks requires it—one must speak with candor and say frankly evil of evil, and blame blamable things; because in doing so, God is glorified. Above all, blame the vice and spare as much as possible the person to whom the vice belongs, all the more so because the goodness of God is so great that a single moment is sufficient for entreating His grace. And who can be sure that the one who yesterday was a sinner, and evil, will be so today?" (SFS, *Thy Will Be Done,* 81).

Prayer: I thank You, Lord Jesus, for seeking to live within me, though I am unworthy. Help me to overcome my human shortcomings, and learn to love and honor everyone as Your special gift.

Wednesday of the Second Week of Advent

Is 40:25–31; Mt 11:28–30

Preparation: Take a few minutes of silence, setting aside all your worries and anxieties, and become aware of the divine presence.

Listening to God's Word: "Come to me, all who labor and are burdened, and I will give you rest. Take my yoke upon you and learn from me, for I am meek and humble of heart; and you will find rest for yourselves" (Mt 11:28–29).

To be refreshed by the Lord

From our daily experiences we know that physical and spiritual weariness is part of our life. Busy schedules make us restless; various problems and difficulties plunge us into deep anxiety and worry; hard work and tough issues in life cause fatigue and tension, leading us to discouragement and frustration. In such situations, we become so exhausted that we seek relief from everything that burdens us. Jesus comes to us in such troubling moments of life, inviting us to take a leap of faith, in trust. Blessed Teresa of Calcutta says, "To be alone with God, not with our books, thoughts, and memories but completely stripped of everything, to dwell lovingly in God's presence—silent, empty, expectant, and motionless. Listen in silence, because if your heart is full of other things you cannot hear the voice of God. But when you have listened to the voice of God in the stillness of your heart, then you can hear God everywhere" (Steve Mueller, *God with Us,* 9). Today, Jesus says to all of us in our struggles, "Come to me, all who labor and are burdened, and I will give you rest" (cf. Mt 11:28). This verse is one of the most celebrated and loved verses in the Bible. It brings us the message of the Lord's comfort and consolation, of His encouragement and personal concern for us. Jesus' message gives us the confidence to believe in God's promise. We are not lost or abandoned because Jesus is always there to inspire and to encourage us, to comfort and guide us through the most difficult and challenging moments of our lives. As Pope Benedict XVI has said, "The Christian faith can never be separated from the soil of sacred events, from the choice made by God, who wanted to speak to us, to become man, to die and rise again, in a particular place and at a particular time."

In our faith-journey, we must realize that before we take the initiative to seek God, He takes the first initiative to defend us, to lift us up after our falls, to comfort us in our weariness and sorrow, and to lead us forward in hope and confidence. Listening to Jesus' voice, and finding peaceful rest, is a learning process. From the school of Jesus, we must acquire the practical wisdom to face courageously all challenging moments and life-threatening events. We need to learn not to give up after our falls or failures, but to rise up with a renewed spirit and refreshed attitude, and to move forward with new hope and optimism. As Isaiah proclaims, "The Lord is the eternal God, creator of the ends of the earth. He does not faint nor grow weary... He gives strength to the fainting; for the weak he makes vigor abound... They that hope in the Lord will renew their strength, they will soar as with eagles' wings; They will run and not grow weary, walk and not grow faint" (Is 40:28–29, 31). Jesus, Who is meek and humble of heart, refreshes us and makes us powerful in our powerlessness. Ask yourself: do I take a leap of faith by entrusting myself to the Lord, in order to be refreshed and renewed by Him? Do I believe in the assurance of Jesus to give me peaceful rest?

Wisdom from St. Francis de Sales: "The uneasiness that you experience at prayer, together with your anxiety to find a subject that can captivate and satisfy your mind, is in itself enough to prevent you from finding what you seek. When we are too intent in our search for something, we can look at it a hundred times without seeing it. Such useless anxiety can only result in weariness of mind which in turn produces this coldness and numbness in your soul. I do think you would gain a great deal if you could keep from being so anxious, for that is one of the greatest obstacles to devotion and real virtue. That is why we have to be on guard against it at all times, especially during prayer" (Marie Thibert, *Letters of Spiritual Direction,* 100).

Prayer: Meek and humble Jesus, thank You for offering me the gift of peaceful rest. Grant me the grace to always seek You in my life, and to follow You in steadfast love till the end.

Thursday of the Second Week of Advent

Is 41:13–20; Mt 11:11–15

Preparation: Take a few minutes of silence, setting aside all your worries and anxieties, and become aware of the divine presence.

Listening to God's Word: "Amen, I say to you, among those born of women there has been none greater than John the Baptist; yet the least in the kingdom of heaven is greater than he. From the days of John the Baptist until now, the kingdom of heaven suffers violence, and the violent are taking it by force" (Mt 11:11–12).

Greatness through faith-filled acceptance

Once, the devil took the form of an angel of light and appeared to one of the holy monks in the desert and said, "I am the angel Gabriel and I have been sent to you by God Almighty." The monk, opening his eyes from his peaceful state of meditation, calmly replied, "You must think again. You must have been sent by God to someone else. I have done nothing great or holy to deserve the visit of an angel." With that the devil vanished from the monk and never again dared to come anywhere near him (De Mello, *Prayer of the Frog,* 180). Today's Gospel narrative highlights two realities: first, the greatness of the least ones in the eyes of God; second, the violence unleashed against God's kingdom and those belonging to it. Saint John the Baptist, by his faithfulness to his vocation and uncompromising prophetic message, proclaimed the imminent coming of the Messiah, by preaching the need for repentance and renewal in life. His lifestyle and prophetic preaching inspired the people of his day. They regarded him as a great prophet, like Elijah, who was expected to return as the forerunner of God's kingdom. Jesus too regarded John as the greatest prophet, but unfortunately, he suffered violent opposition and was locked in the prison. However, Jesus announced that the least and the insignificant believers will be great because of their uncompromising faith in Him and accepting God's kingdom in total surrender. All such people believe in the promise of the Messianic age ushered in by Jesus' actions that God comes to save the people, though they are insignificant and valueless in the eyes of the world. For God says, "I am the Lord, your God. Fear not, I will help you"

(Is 41:13). This is the marvelous work that God does for us through Jesus the Messiah.

Blessed Teresa of Calcutta says, “Give yourself fully to God who will use you to accomplish great things on the condition that you believe much more in God’s love than in your weakness. If we really entirely belong to God, then we must be at His disposal and trust in Him. Being happy with God means this: to love as He loves, to help as He helps, to give as He gives and to serve as He serves” (Mueller, *God with Us*, 14). By relying on God in total trust, we must be prepared to face the challenges and hardships posed by the violent oppositions of our world that would provoke or force us to compromise our faith-values. The prophets of the Old Testament, Saint John the Baptist, and Jesus Himself, faced violent opposition during their lifetimes. The early Church, too, was challenged by violent opposition; and it happens in our times as well. On all such occasions, we must be uncompromising and unrelenting like John the Baptist, always believing that our God comes to protect and guide us through all hardships. Therefore let us remember that “Advent is the perfect time to clear and prepare the way. Advent is a winter training camp for those who desire peace. By reflection and prayer, we can make our hearts a place where a blessing of peace would desire to abide and where the birth of the Prince of Peace might take place” (Edward Hays). Ask yourself: what can I do this Advent to follow the Lord in faithfulness, and to trust Him even in the face of challenges? Do I hear Jesus telling me, “I am the Lord and I will not forsake you”?

Wisdom from St. Francis de Sales: “Let us do three things and we shall have peace; let us have a very pure intention of seeking, in all things, the honor and glory of God; let us do the little we can toward this end, and let us leave to God the care of all the rest. Why does anyone who has God for the object of his intentions and who is doing the best he can, let himself be disturbed? No. God is not so frightening to those He loves. He is content with little because He knows very well that we don’t have much. You must know that our Lord is the Prince of Peace (Is 9:5) and He holds everything in peace” (Marie Thibert, *Letters of Spiritual Direction,* 119).

Prayer: Thank You, Jesus, for revealing God as a loving Father. Grant me Your grace to accept the Father’s will and face in trust all trials and struggles so that I may remain loyal to You.

Friday of the Second Week of Advent

Is 48:17–19; Mt 11:16–19

Preparation: Take a few minutes of silence, setting aside all your worries and anxieties, and become aware of the divine presence.

Listening to God's Word: "For John came neither eating nor drinking, and they said, 'He is possessed by a demon.' The Son of Man came eating and drinking and they said, 'Look, He is a glutton and a drunkard, a friend of tax collectors and sinners'" (Mt 11:18–19).

Listening to God's call

Once, there was a preacher who kept saying, "The essential thing we all must do is that we must put God first in our lives." To him the spiritual Master said, "There is no need for it. He is already there. Our business is to recognize him, listen to him and faithfully follow him." As described in the Gospel narrative, Jesus was disappointed by the fickleness of the people because they deliberately rejected the prophetic call of Saint John the Baptist to repent and they also failed to appreciate and accept His acts of salvation. John was true to his prophetic call and set a model for the people by his simple and ascetic lifestyle. Yet some people regarded him as possessed and ignored him, since his message about the coming judgment was too threatening and his approach otherworldly. Jesus was joyful and sociable, interacting with everyone, showing love and compassion to all; yet the same people labeled Him as a drunkard and friend of sinners (cf. Mt 11:19) who was not spiritual enough. This shows the childish dissatisfaction and mean-spiritedness of the people, which resulted in their refusal to accept the message of repentance and renewal. A certain Sage once said, "Do you listen to God speaking within you and around you? When you hear him speaking to you, you become awakened." God speaks to us through Isaiah: "If you would hearken to my commandments, your prosperity would be like a river, and your vindication like the waves of the sea; your descendants would be like the sand and those born of your stock like its grains, their name never cut off or blotted out from my presence" (Is 48:18–19).

The rejection experienced by John and Jesus can help us, as a believing community, to deal with the rejection and opposition we may experience in our own times. We do not need to be discouraged or disheartened in such moments; rather, it should lead us to a deeper conviction of our faith-values and encourage us to be vigorous witnesses to Jesus. Such experiences also remind us that to follow the way of Jesus is to follow His law of love, which means responding to the call of conversion. Henri Nouwen says, "Praying is first and foremost listening to Jesus who dwells in the very depths of your heart. Whatever you do with your life, go on listening to the voice of Jesus in your heart. This listening must be an active and very attentive listening which will help you to know Jesus in a very intimate way, make you aware of the unique manner in which he is calling you, and give you the courage to follow him even to places where you would rather not go" (Mueller, *God with Us*, 15). Discipleship inevitably entails wholehearted listening to God and living a life according to His words, with a change of heart that involves a new perspective and renewed attitudes in life. A saying of wonderful wisdom goes like this: "Take time to be aware that in the very midst of our busy preparations for the celebration of Christ's birth in ancient Bethlehem, Christ is reborn in the Bethlehems of our homes and daily lives. Take time, slow down, be still, be awake to the Divine Mystery that looks so common and so ordinary yet is wondrously present" (Edward Hays). Therefore, let us come to Jesus with an attitude of sincere listening, that we may discern His plan of human salvation and follow Him faithfully within our own life situations. Ask yourself: can I take a little more time to pray for the graces needed to overcome the hurdles and trials in my life of discipleship? Do I listen to Jesus, and accept in faith His words and actions revealing God's reign?

Wisdom from St. Francis de Sales: "If we are able to speak to our Lord, let us do so; let us praise Him, pray to Him, listen to Him. If we are unable to speak because our voice fails us, let us, nevertheless, stay in the hall of the king and bow down before Him. He will see us there, will graciously accept our patience, and look with favor on our silence. Another time we will be very surprised when He takes us by the hand, chats with us, and walks with us up and down in His garden of prayer; and even if He never does this, let us be satisfied that it is our duty to be in His entourage and that it's a great grace and still greater honor that He allows us to be in his presence" (Marie Thibert, *Letters of Spiritual Direction,* 101).

Prayer: Thank You, Jesus, for Your words of hope and encouragement. Help me to listen to Your voice and walk with You in faith so that I may be able to find true happiness in life.

Saturday of the Second Week of Advent

Sir 48:1–4, 9–11; Mt 17:9a, 10–13

Preparation: Take a few minutes of silence, setting aside all your worries and anxieties, and become aware of the divine presence.

Listening to God's Word: "Then the disciples asked Him, 'Why do the scribes say that Elijah must come first?' He said in reply, 'Elijah will indeed come and restore all things; but I tell you that Elijah has already come, and they did not recognize him but did to him whatever they pleased. So also will the Son of Man suffer at their hands'" (Mt 17:10–12).

Recognizing Jesus

Once, a man of faith asked the spiritual master, "Where shall I look for enlightenment?" "Here," said the master. "When will it happen?" "It is happening right now." "Then why don't I experience it?" "Because you do not look." "What should I look for?" "Nothing. Just look." "Look at what?" "Anything your eyes alight upon." "Must I look in a special kind of way?" "No. The ordinary way will do." "But don't I always look the ordinary way?" "No." "Why not?" "Because to look you must be here in the present. You are mostly somewhere else distracted." (De Mello, *One Minute Wisdom,* 12). As we read in Scripture, the scribes taught that Elijah would come before the final day of the Lord to restore the covenant and make everything ready (cf. Mal 3:23–26; 4:5–6). It was believed that He would reestablish unity within the tribes of Israel. Therefore, Elijah symbolized a total transformation of the house of Israel through God's intervention (cf. Sir 48:9–11). However, when he was with the people, preaching God's word, they did not accept him. When Saint John the Baptist came, preaching a message of repentance and renewal to prepare the way for the Messiah, he also was rejected. Jesus, the Messiah Himself, came and He too had to suffer the fate of the prophets because the people refused to accept Him (cf. Mt 17:12). Jesus' Incarnation is the eschatological event that marked the decisive moment of God's intervention in salvation history. If we acknowledge Jesus and accept Him in our midst, we will certainly receive messianic blessings through Him.

Elijah was a catalyst for the promotion of reconciliation and forgiveness among the Israelites, who were God's chosen people. Jesus and Saint John the Baptist preached about a personal change of heart and spiritual renewal. Jesus came to redeem us and reconcile us with the Father, and we are called to go through the process of personal renewal as preparation for celebrating the Messiah's birth. Jesus continues the saving act of forgiveness and reconciliation through His involvement and life-giving presence in our lives. Elijah's return, which was expected to restore all things; the preaching of Saint John the Baptist; and the arrival of Jesus as the Messiah, all reaffirm the redemptive hope that God has not abandoned humanity or creation as a whole, but still acts decisively, that we may be redeemed at the *eschaton*. The eschatological redemption of the world is already unfolded and present among us in Jesus who calls us to make a concrete decision by our change of heart for a renewed life. God says, "For the sake of my name I restrain my anger, for the sake of my renown I hold it back from you, lest I should destroy you. See, I have refined you like silver, tested you in the furnace of affliction" (Is 48:19–11). Pope Benedict XVI said that "Advent is concerned with that very connection between memory and hope which is so necessary to man. Advent's intention is to awaken the most profound memory within us, namely, the memory of the God who became a child. This healing memory brings us hope." Ask yourself: am I aware of Jesus' life-giving presence in my own life experiences? How am I prepared to receive messianic blessings in this Advent season?

Wisdom from St. Francis de Sales: "There is a real temptation to become dissatisfied with the world and depressed about it when we must be in it. God's providence is wiser than we are. We imagine we would feel better if we were on another ship; that may be, but only if we change ourselves! I am the sworn enemy of all those useless, dangerous, unwise desires, for even if what we desire is good, the desiring itself is pointless since God does not want that kind of good for us, but another, toward which He expects us to strive. He might wish to speak to us from the thorny bush as He did to Moses [Ex 3:2], when we expect Him to speak to us from the gentle breeze as He did to Elijah [1Kgs 19:12]" (Marie Thibert, *Letters of Spiritual Direction,* 162).

Prayer: Jesus my Savior, stir up with Your grace my inner longing for peace and reconciliation. Enlighten me, that I may recognize You in my brothers and sisters, and live in fraternal love.

Third Week - Joy

"The happiness you are seeking, the happiness
You have a right to enjoy has a name and a face:
It is Jesus of Nazareth, hidden in the Eucharist;
Only He gives the fullness of life to humanity!"
(Pope Benedict XVI)

Monday of the Third Week of Advent

Num 24:2–7, 15–17; Mt 21:23–27

Preparation: Take a few minutes of silence, setting aside all your worries and anxieties, and become aware of the divine presence.

Listening to God's Word: "When He had come into the temple area, the chief priests and the elders of the people approached Him as He was teaching and said, 'By what authority are you doing these things? And who gave you this authority?' Jesus said to them in reply, 'I shall ask you one question, and if you answer it for me, then I shall tell you by what authority I do these things'" (Mt 21:23–24).

The authority of Jesus

Once, a prophet came to a city to convert its inhabitants. At first the people earnestly listened to his sermons, but they gradually drifted away from him till there was not even a single person to hear the prophet's preaching. But he continued to preach. So a traveler asked him, "Why do you go on preaching when no one is interested to listen to you?" The prophet replied, "In the beginning I hoped to change these people through my sermon but I failed. If I still keep preaching, it is only to prevent them from changing me" (Anthony de Mello, *Song of the Bird*, 59). Jesus' teachings and healing activities were powerful enough to affect and influence people. Yet, as narrated in the Gospel account today, the religious leaders always critiqued Jesus' actions and questioned His authority (Mt 21:23). Their motive was not to know the genuineness of Jesus' authority; rather, they tried to force Him into public admission that He was from God and that His authority came directly from God, so that they could trap Him with the charge of blasphemy. But Jesus responded to the religious leaders with a counter-question about Saint John the Baptist's authority to preach. The background for this reference was the popular enthusiasm which John the Baptist aroused among the people of his time. Josephus, the Jewish historian, says that "his sermons aroused the highest degree of enthusiasm among people. Consequently many others joined his movement. So Herod became alarmed and worried because it seemed that they could be guided by John in everything they did" (Daniel J. Harrington, *Sacra Pagina: The Gospel of Matthew,* 300).

The chief priests and the elders of the people, who constituted the Jewish leadership (the Sanhedrin) in Jerusalem, and whose lives centered on the temple, worked alongside the Roman officials as well as Herod Antipas to maintain peace, order and security. Therefore John's movement posed not only religious but also political threats. When the question arose, the religious leaders were afraid to make a judgment concerning John the Baptist. Jesus, by His counter-question, indirectly affirmed that just as John's authority to preach came from God, Jesus also had His authority from God to preach and do works of healing. However, He never used His power and authority for self-glorification or to gain public honor; but only for proclaiming God's reign and preaching about God's love and compassion. Henry Nouwen points out, "Jesus is the revelation of God's unending, unconditional love for us human beings. Everything that Jesus has done, said, and undergone is meant to show that the love we most long for is given to us by God—not because we have deserved it, but because God is a God of love. What God asks us is to have faith in that love. When Jesus talks about faith, He means first of all to trust unreservedly that we are loved by God" (from James E. Adams, *Living Hope,* 13). Jesus was obedient to the Father in His authoritative preaching and healing activities, and He faithfully fulfilled the Divine plan for the salvation of the world. Ask yourself: as a believer, do I use my power and authority for my self-glorification and honor, or for serving God's people? Do I fulfill my responsibilities as an opportunity to reveal Jesus, or assert my authority for self-interests?

Wisdom from St. Francis de Sales: "Certainly, in the Incarnation He has made us see that which otherwise the human mind could hardly have imagined or understood, that is, that God was man and man God: the immortal, mortal; the one incapable of suffering, suffering—subject to heat, cold, hunger and thirst; the infinite, finite; the eternal, temporal—in short, man divinized and God humanized in such a way that God, without ceasing to be God, is man; and man, without ceasing to be man, is God" (Visitation, *The Sermons of SFS for Advent and Christmas,* 71-72).

Prayer: Loving Jesus, thank You for teaching me to do the Father's will. Help me to overcome my attitudes of self-sufficiency and authoritarianism in order to serve others in fraternal love.

Tuesday of the Third Week of Advent

Zeph 3:1–2, 9–13; Mt 21:28–32

Preparation: Take a few minutes of silence, setting aside all your worries and anxieties, and become aware of the divine presence.

Listening to God's Word: "What is your opinion? A man had two sons. He came to the first and said, 'Son, go out and work in the vineyard today.' He said in reply, 'I will not,' but afterwards he changed his mind and went. The man came to the other son and gave the same order. He said in reply, 'Yes, sir,' but did not go. Which of the two did his father's will?" (Mt 21:28–31).

Positive response in faith

When children say no to their parents' requests or instruction, the parents become angry and upset. The teachers will be upset and disgusted with the students when they refuse to obey or misbehave. Today's Gospel parable reminds us of the crucial moment of our faith-response to Jesus, either positively or negatively. Once, a famous scholar came to the Master seeking guidance. "What is it that you seek?" asked the Master. "Life," was the scholar's reply. The Master said, "If you are to live happily, words must die." "What does that mean?" asked the scholar. The Master replied, "You are lost and forlorn because you dwell in a world of words. You feed on words, you are satisfied with words while forgetting that what you need is substance. A menu will not satisfy your hunger. A mere formula will not quench your thirst." Following Jesus does not consist in merely boasting about one's faith or speaking eloquent words but in living concretely by one's faith-convictions. We know that actions speak louder than words. The striking point of today's Gospel parable is the contrasting response of the two sons: they each said one thing, but did not act accordingly. The first son in the parable responded negatively to his father's order, but later he changed his mind and obeyed his father (Mt 21:29–30); whereas the second son responded positively to his father's order, but did not obey it (v. 31).

The parable is directed toward the Jewish religious leaders of the time, who were compared to the son who said "yes" to the father but did not carry out his order. The first son's negative answer to his father's request reflected his human character of unsteadiness in conviction. Nevertheless, when he changed his mind later, it shows that a process of personal reflection and self-evaluation had taken place within him. In that process, he was open to a renewal that changed his whole attitude, making all the difference in his life. As a result, he responded positively, with personal conviction, and fulfilled his father's command. This is how those marginal people, who were regarded as outcasts and sinners in society, accepted the invitation of Saint John the Baptist and Jesus: by welcoming their preaching with openness of mind, ready for renewal. Consequently, they gained the first place in God's kingdom. However, the religious leaders of the day, who claimed to be the righteous ones, refused to respond positively to the prophets or to Jesus Himself. The prophet Zephaniah had once reproached such an attitude of the people saying, "She [Jerusalem] hears no voice, accepts no correction. In the Lord, she has not trusted, to her God she has not drawn near" (Zeph 3:2). Jeremiah says, "This nation does not listen to the voice of its God or take correction. Faithfulness has disappeared from her" (Jer 7:28). It is always easy to say "yes" to the Lord in the first instance due to enthusiasm and eagerness; but then it becomes challenging to live by our "yes," especially in moments of hardship. Ask yourself: can I accept my human frailties and shortcomings and persevere in going through the process of renewal and change? Do I courageously embark on a new course of action, ready to follow Jesus with a positive response of faith, by saying *yes* to Him in all moments of life?

Wisdom from St. Francis de Sales: "In fact, there is no other art than to set ourselves to the work of loving God, applying ourselves to the practice of those things that are pleasing to Him. This is the only means of finding and acquiring this holy love, provided that this practice is undertaken in simplicity, without trouble or solicitude. Simplicity embraces all the means that are prescribed to each of us, according to his vocation, for acquiring the love of God. The virtue of simplicity concerns the pure love of God which is its single and only aim" (SFS, *The Art of Loving God,* 108).

Prayer: My Gentle Jesus! You love the poor and mercifully hear their cry. Grant me a compassionate heart, that I may love and honor people with dignity and always say "yes" to Your call.

Wednesday of the Third Week of Advent

Is 45:6c–8, 18, 21c–25; Lk 7:18b–23

Preparation: Take a few minutes of silence, setting aside all your worries and anxieties, and become aware of the divine presence.

Listening to God's Word: "John summoned two of his disciples and sent them to the Lord to ask, 'Are you the one who is to come or should we look for another?' At that time he cured many of their diseases, sufferings, and evil spirits; he also granted sight to many who were blind. And he said to them in reply, 'Go and tell John what you have seen and heard'" (Lk 7:18–19, 21-22).

The mission of the Messiah

The prophets of the Old Testament foretold certain signs that would take place to herald the coming of the Messiah (cf. Is 35:4–6). As presented in today's Gospel narrative, Jesus, through His healing miracles, presented Himself as the long-awaited Messiah who was ushering in the messianic era. As the Messiah, Jesus brought liberation to people by offering them healing and wholeness (Lk 7:22). Thus, Jesus has united all broken lines, and gathered all scattered sounds into harmony. As Pope Francis says, "Even when sin broke off our relationship with God, others, and creation, God didn't abandon us. The history of salvation is the story of God who seeks out human beings, offers them His love, and welcomes them." This is the mission of Jesus. However, the question from the disciples of John is intriguing. Why did he send the disciples to Jesus with such a question? Did he doubt that Jesus was the expected Messiah? It is a commonly accepted opinion that John directed his disciples to ask this question so that they would hear, from the mouth of Jesus Himself, that He was the Messiah that was foretold by the prophets and witnessed to by John. It is not that John doubted Jesus to be the Messiah; rather, he wanted his disciples to have firsthand experience of who Jesus was and of His mission, so that they would believe in him.

The Master once asked the disciples, "When will you recognize that the day has dawned and identify the light from darkness?" One disciple said, "If we are able to identify clearly a tiger at a distance to be a real tiger, then we can say that the day has dawned." "No," the Master said. Another one said, "If we can recognize a tree at a distance clearly to be a mango tree or a banyan tree, then we can say that the day has dawned." "No," the Master said again. The disciples could not give the right answer. They were confused, and so they asked, "When can we then recognize the day and see the light?" "When you are able to see in others your own brothers and sisters, the day has dawned for you and you can see the light. Until then you are in darkness," the Master said. Jesus saw the image of the Father in everyone and loved them compassionately. As disciples of Jesus, our compassionate approach, along with our loving and caring attitude toward others (especially toward those who are less privileged) can proclaim the messianic era of Jesus in our world, and assure others that God loves us, even at our worst. Vincent Van Gogh said that "the best way to know God is to love many things: love a friend, a wife, something good in life, whatever you like...that people will know there is a God who cares for them, and will surely believe in such a God." John showed his disciples the door of hope to find Jesus the Messiah. By our faith-filled acts of love and kindness, we can bring the words of Isaiah to fulfillment: "Let the earth open and salvation bud forth; let justice also spring up" (Is 45:8). "We need the eyes of deep faith to see Christ in the broken body and dirty clothes under which the most beautiful one among the sons of men hides. We need the hand of Christ to touch those bodies wounded by pain and suffering" (Blessed Teresa of Calcutta). Ask yourself: during this Advent, am I able to see others as my brothers and sisters? Can I speak words of appreciation and kindle the light of hope in the lives of people around me?

Wisdom from St. Francis de Sales: "The glorious St. John the Baptist did not send his disciples to Jesus our Lord to find out whether or not He was the Messiah. He had three reasons for sending those disciples to Jesus. First, to make Him known to the whole world. He had already spent time preaching His coming, His miracles, and His greatness to his disciples. Now he wanted them to see Him whom he had announced to them. Second, he did not want to draw disciples to himself but only to his Teacher that in His school they might be instructed personally by Him. The third reason is to detach them from himself and let them see the miracles that Jesus Christ performed so that they might come to Him in a manner worthy of Him" (Visitation, *The Sermons of SFS for Advent and Christmas,* 5-7).

Prayer: Jesus my Savior, thank You for inaugurating the blessings of the Messianic age. Help me to bring Your blessings to others through acts of kindness, welcoming everyone with love.

Thursday of the Third Week of Advent

Is 54:1–10; Lk 7:24–30

Preparation: Take a few minutes of silence, setting aside all your worries and anxieties, and become aware of the divine presence.

Listening to God's Word: "When the messengers of John had left, Jesus began to speak to the crowds about John. 'What did you go out to the desert to see—a reed swayed by the wind?… I tell you, among those born of women, no one is greater than John; yet the least in the kingdom of God is greater than he.' All the people, who listened, including the tax collectors, and who were baptized with the baptism of John, acknowledged the righteousness of God" (Lk 7:24, 28–29).

Rejection or re-orientation

Clinging to our failures and justifying our wrong decisions will lead us to make more mess and new mistakes; but learning life lessons from failures and faults can reorient us to live our present life happily and meaningfully. This is the point of Jesus' teaching in today's Gospel. Once, a group of disciples went on a pilgrimage to different shrines, and the Master gave them some bitter herbs and said, "Take these herbs along with you and make sure that you dip them into the holy water in all the shrines and get them blessed." The disciples also did exactly as the Master had asked them. When they returned, the bitter herbs were cooked and served as sacramental food. After tasting the sacred food, the Master said, "Strange. The holy waters and the blessing from so many sacred shrines could not sweeten the bitter herbs." Strictly observing some religious traditions and practicing certain rituals alone will not lead us to personal renewal or to closer union with God; instead, we are to live in love by accepting God's will in trust. The tax collectors and those baptized by Saint John the Baptist, learning from their own faults and sins, reoriented their life purpose and acknowledged God's righteousness (cf. Lk 7:29). Though once they did not understand or accept God's plan, they later listened to God's call and renewed their lives. Nevertheless the religious leaders such as the Pharisees and the scholars of the law, who proclaimed themselves to be the pious ones and the guardians of religious tradition, rejected God's plan by deliberately rejecting Jesus and His teachings (cf. v. 30).

At times, God can come into our life with compassion and mercy, speaking tenderly; other times God can speak to us sternly, with an uncompromising prophetic voice, leading us to self-examination. If we want to experience God in our life, we must first allow God to find us, and, in faith, we must discern God's plans for us. Those who listened to God's voice—through prophets such as Saint John the Baptist and through Jesus Himself—accepted God's righteousness and reoriented their lives. In the Book of Isaiah it is explained that although God abandoned Israel for her faults and remained silent, yet He renewed the covenant to show His unconditional love and to protect and restore Israel (cf. Is 54:6–10). The Incarnation of Jesus is the fulfillment of this promise of God to humanity. In fact, our human life is a constant Advent season wherein we are continually waiting to become; to discover; to grow; and to fulfill all our dreams and aspirations. Our hope-filled desires, life-struggles, fears, frustrations, expectations, and fulfillments are all part of the Advent experience. The world is not as just and loving as we usually expect it to be. Yet, the Incarnation of Jesus Christ gives us a reason to live in the hope that Jesus the light will shatter the darkness of our world; and that we can be liberated from our fears and prejudices. In this Advent season, our interior attitude must be to welcome Jesus and accept God's will on God's own terms, and not according to our own likes and dislikes. Ask yourself: do I take pride in my self-righteousness and reject God's plan, or do I listen to God's call and reorient my life's purpose? Do I see God's hand in every circumstance of my life?

Wisdom from St. Francis de Sales: "This is the grace I desire for you, my dear souls, that you remain very near to this sacred Savior who is about to gather us all around Himself in order to keep us always under the standard of His most holy protection, just like the shepherd who has care of his sheep and of his flock. May His goodness grant us the grace to hear His voice so that in recognizing Him as our sovereign Shepherd we will not stray away nor listen to the voice of the stranger who remains near us like an infernal wolf (1 Pet 5:8). May we have the fidelity to keep ourselves submissive, obedient and subject to His wishes and commands in order that we might begin in this life what we shall do eternally in heaven" (Visitation, *The Sermons of SFS for Advent and Christmas,* 61).

Prayer: Jesus my Redeemer, grant me Your grace to prepare myself by reorienting my life-purpose, so that I will be ever ready to welcome you, in faith and trust, at Your daily coming.

Friday of the Third Week of Advent

Is 56:1–3, 6–8; Jn 5:33–36

Preparation: Take a few minutes of silence, setting aside all your worries and anxieties, and become aware of the divine presence.

Listening to God's Word: "You sent emissaries to John, and he testified to the truth. He was a burning and shining lamp, and for a while you were content to rejoice in his light. But I have testimony greater than John's. The works that the Father gave me to accomplish, these works that I perform testify on my behalf that the Father has sent me" (Jn 5:33, 35–36).

Testifying to the Truth

In our common legal system, there must be verifiable evidence as a witness to prove or disprove the truth about a case. According to the Jewish practice of the time, it was not enough for the accused one to provide evidence for the truth regarding certain facts. There needed to be at least two witnesses, whose word could be trusted. Though Jesus claimed God the Father as a witness for His actions (cf. Jn 5:37), it was not enough for the Jews, since this witness could not be verified. So Jesus turned to Saint John the Baptist, who as a shining light witnessed to the coming Messiah, Jesus the Truth. Secondly, Jesus presents His own works (this refers to His entire ministry) as a perfect fulfillment of God's plan for human salvation (cf. Jn 5:36b). Such a faithful accomplishment of His ministry proves Jesus' divine origin. Thus, Jesus, as the Messiah, proved His identity as the Son of God by faithfully carrying out the works of the Father. He never failed on that account but fulfilled this task, even to death. A seeker once heard a loud knocking in his heart. "Who is there?" asked the frightened seeker. "It is I, the Truth," came the answer. The seeker said, "Don't be ridiculous. Truth speaks only in silence." That effectively stopped the knocking, to the great relief of the seeker. What the poor man did not know was that the knocking in his heart was produced by the fearful beating of his heart. The truth that sets us free is almost always the Truth we would rather not hear. So when we say that something isn't true, we frequently mean to say, "I don't like it" (De Mello, *Prayer of the Frog*, 270).

Saint John the Baptist, as a shining lamp, testified to Jesus the Truth—but he suffered a violent death. Jesus the Messiah witnessed by His life and works to the Truth about the Father's love and gift of salvation to all—yet He was hated, and suffered crucifixion on account of the Truth to which He testified. As followers of Jesus, how faithful and committed are we to fulfilling the tasks and responsibilities entrusted to us? We can daily make an Advent examination: are there any feelings of discrimination in us toward a particular race, sex, cast, region or religion? Is there a lingering resentment, an unforgiven injury, living in our hearts? Do we look down upon others of lesser social standing or educational achievement? Are we respectful of others' ideas and needs? Such questions can become Advent lights by which we may search deeply the dark corners of our hearts. The task of testifying to the truth will not be that easy. It will be, most of the time, very challenging and troublesome, yet satisfying and fruit-bearing. Though speaking contrary to our faith-values and to the truth might be easier and convenient, it will be troublemaking and unrewarding, creating crises and meaninglessness in life. Isaiah says, "Observe what is right, do what is just; for my salvation is about to come, my justice, about to be revealed. Happy is the man who does this, the son of man who holds to it; Who keeps the Sabbath free from profanation, and his hand from any evildoing" (Is 56:1–2). Ask yourself: in my life of faith, do I hear the voices of the prophets, and give witness to Jesus the Truth by a life of honesty and sincerity? Am I interested in knowing the truth and living by it, or do I distort it according to my convenience?

Wisdom from St. Francis de Sales: "Now how are we to pronounce the sacred name of Jesus so that it may be beneficial and profitable to us? This name certainly ought not to be pronounced carelessly or thoughtlessly. It is not enough to be aware that it is a two-syllable word, nor even less to speak it merely with the mouth. Our Lord shed His blood in receiving His name. In that He indicated His willingness to do what this holy name signifies: to save. Therefore, it must be engraved upon your heart. How happy we will be if, at the hour of our death, as well as during the whole of our lives, we pronounce the sacred name of the Savior with due respect and love. It will be like a password by which we will freely enter Heaven, for it is the name of our redemption" (Visitation, *The Sermons of SFS for Advent and Christmas,* 100-101).

Prayer: My loving Jesus, you are the Way, the Truth, and the Life. Guide me that I may follow you in faithfulness, and witness to the truth about the Father's love, even in the face of hardships.

Fourth Week - Love

"There is no other art than to set ourselves
To the work of loving God, applying ourselves to
The practice of those things that are pleasing to him;
This is the only means of finding and acquiring
This holy love."

(St. Francis de Sales)

December 17th

Gen 49:2, 8–10; Mt 1:1–17

Preparation: Take a few minutes of silence, setting aside all your worries and anxieties, and become aware of the divine presence.

Listening to God's Word: "Abraham became the father of Isaac, Isaac the father of Jacob, Jacob the father of Judah and his brothers. …Jacob the father of Joseph, the husband of Mary. Of her was born Jesus who is called the Messiah" (Mt 1:2, 16).

The family tree of Jesus

Family is very important to all of us, and we truly appreciate the gift of our family bond of love and affection. All of us are somehow influenced, and our behaviors formed, by our family's values. Therefore, Saint John XXIII had said that "mankind is a great, an immense family. This is proved by what we feel in our hearts at Christmas." Saint Matthew, by offering the family tree of Jesus at the beginning of his Gospel, shows the historical link of Jesus the Messiah to the ancestors and descendents of David (cf. 1:1–17), beginning with Abraham. We also have a similar account of Jesus' family tree in the Gospel of Saint Luke, though with a few differences. Luke presents the family tree of Jesus at the beginning of His ministry, starting with Jesus the Messiah and going all the way back to Adam, the first man. This is to show the divine origin and divine Sonship of Jesus, and the universal character of God's salvation (cf. Lk 3:23–38). However, Matthew illustrates, through this genealogy, a solid foundation for the claim of Jesus that He is a descendent of David. By explaining the ancestral history of Jesus, Matthew taught the Jewish Christians that Jesus is the expected Messiah, ruling from the Davidic dynasty, and is related to Abraham, their father in faith. Matthew strongly teaches that the promise of God to Abraham that he would be a blessing for the world (cf. Gen 12:2–3) is fulfilled in Jesus. The relation between the old Israel and the new Israel is firmly built up and the faith-journey of Abraham in the Old Testament (cf. Gen 12:1, 4–6), as well as the faith-journey of Mary in the New Testament (cf. Lk 1:26–38) are inter-related. Thus, the genealogy of Jesus proves that He was a historical person, Who actually lived and died to bring about human salvation. However, we can see from Jesus' genealogy that pagans and sinners, too, had their role among the righteous in fulfilling the divine plan for human salvation. Even adverse events such as the Babylonian exile advanced God's plan.

As believers, we must realize that we have our own roles to play in God's plan. However, we should not be too comfortable in our conviction that God's plan will always be to our liking, because when our unfounded hopes and dreams lead us into new and unexpected directions, we may be too easily jolted by despair and frustration. Therefore, we should keep our hearts always open to God's will, as Joseph and Mary did. Then we will learn to understand and appreciate God's plan for us, which will lead us to many unexpected blessings. By celebrating Jesus' Incarnation, we in fact celebrate and experience the nearness of God among us as well as our belonging to God and God's belonging to us. Pope Francis says, "Remain steadfast in the journey of faith with the firm hope in the Lord. He gives us the courage to swim against the current." Joseph and Mary experienced God's love and had deep faith in following God's plan in their life. In our Advent preparations, we should learn, from the family tree of Jesus, to develop a deep sense of family-belonging—founded on God's love and revealed in Jesus our Savior—by loving and honoring one another as brothers and sisters. Ask yourself: how do I discern and accept God's plan for me within my own life situations? Do I cooperate with God's plan in sincerity of heart, or distort it according to my liking? How do I serve as an instrument of God's blessings for others?

Wisdom from St. Francis de Sales: "Do faithfully all the things you have to do, but be aware that what matters most is your salvation and the fulfillment of that salvation through true devotion. I don't want a devotion that is bizarre, confused, neurotic, strained, and sad, but rather, a gentle, attractive, peaceful piety; in a word, a piety that is quite spontaneous and wins the love of God and the love of others. Be His and at every minute offer and give your heart to God, long for Him, and make your devotion pleasing and joyful" (Marie Thibert, *Letters of Spiritual Direction,* 156, 159).

Prayer: God, my loving Father, thank You for creating me as part of Your human family. Help me to appreciate and promote family values, and love everyone in fraternal solidarity.

December 18th

Jer 23:5–8; Mt 1:18–25

Preparation: Take a few minutes of silence, setting aside all your worries and anxieties, and become aware of the divine presence.

Listening to God's Word: "Joseph her husband, since he was a righteous man, yet unwilling to expose her to shame, decided to divorce her quietly. Such was his intention when, behold, the angel of the Lord appeared to him in a dream and said, 'Joseph, son of David, do not be afraid to take Mary your wife into your home.' When Joseph awoke, he did as the angel of the Lord had commanded him and took his wife into his home" (Mt 1:19–20, 24).

A person of righteousness

From our common human experiences, we have seen that people divorce or separate for even petty reasons such as resentment, argument, and misunderstanding. As presented in today's Gospel account, Joseph stands as a model for all of us, an encouragement for us to show fairness and kindness toward others by following the Gospel teachings of Jesus. In the Old Testament, a just man is presented as the one who listens to God's word, and lives according to the divine will, faithfully fulfilling the law (cf. Psalms 37:26, 29; 64:11; 68:4). Once, a man of spiritual repute came to the Master and said, "I cannot pray, I cannot understand the Scriptures, I cannot do the exercises that I prescribe to others, I cannot concentrate on my meditation." "Then give them all up and don't bother about them," said the Master cheerfully. "But how can I give them up? I am supposed to be a holy man and have a great following of people in this place," the man replied. The Master said with a sigh, "Holiness today for people like you is only a mere name without a reality in life. But truly holiness is genuine only when it is a reality without a name," (De Mello, *One Minute Wisdom*, 198). The Psalmist says, "Lord, who may abide in your tent? Whoever walks without blame, doing what is right, speaking truth from the heart; who does not slander a neighbor, does no harm to another, never defames a friend" (Ps 15:1–3). Such a person is the ideal human person through his wisdom and kindness. Joseph exemplifies such a person of righteousness and faithfulness. That is why he could not even think of hurting others or putting others to shame and humiliation. This was the true character of Joseph and so "He did not wish to put Mary into disgrace" (Mt 1:19).

By most human standards, people do not believe in their dreams and act accordingly; but Joseph believed the revelation of God in his own dreams, and made the decision to support and protect Mary. In making such a hard decision, he performed a lot of sacrifices. He gave up his freedom of choice, his personal interests, and marital relations. He indeed faced baffling and painful enigmas. By accepting Mary with her conception by the Holy Spirit, and after a soul-searching puzzlement, Joseph surrendered to God's will and firmly resolved to cooperate with God's salvific plan as much as Mary did. This shows his tremendous faith in God and his courage in facing all hardships that might come his way. This reveals his faith-conviction and spiritual maturity. Here, Joseph is an inspiration for all of us—but especially for married couples—to commit themselves to live for each other's happiness, and not to bring disgrace to one another. We are called to be witnesses of God's love, by the love we extend to others; precursors of God's justice, by our unfailing commitment to what is right and good; lamps reflecting the light of the Messiah, by our forgiveness, mercy and compassion; harvesters of souls, through our humble and dedicated service to others. Ask yourself: do I learn like Joseph to grow in my faith and surrender to do God's plan? Do I bring happiness to others, or cause them disgrace and humiliation by my actions and behaviors?

Wisdom from St. Francis de Sales: "Here is the most important point: find out what God wants, and when you know, try to carry it out cheerfully or at least courageously; not only that, but you must love this will of God and the obligations it entails, even if it means performing the most menial tasks in the world the rest of your life, because whatever sauce God chooses for us, it should be all the same to us. In this practice lies the very bull's-eye of perfection at which we must all aim, and whoever comes nearest to it wins the prize. But be of good heart, I beg you; little by little train your will to follow God's will, wherever it may lead you" (Marie Thibert, *Letters of Spiritual Direction,* 109).

Prayer: God our loving Father, thank You for inspiring me by Saint Joseph's faithful witness. Guide me to cooperate with Your divine plan, so that I may bring others blessings and not disgrace.

December 19th

Jgs 13:2–7, 24–25a; Lk 1:5–25

Preparation: Take a few minutes of silence, setting aside all your worries and anxieties, and become aware of the divine presence.

Listening to God's Word: "There was a priest named Zechariah of the priestly division of Abijah; his wife was from the daughters of Aaron, and her name was Elizabeth. Both were righteous in the eyes of God, observing all the commandments and ordinances of the Lord blamelessly. But they had no child, because Elizabeth was barren and both were advanced in years" (Lk 1:5–7).

God's power in human impossibility

When others look down on us because of our lack of fortune or success in life, we feel ashamed and humiliated. When married women, in particular, come to know of their barrenness, they become devastated, and feel humiliated in the eyes of society. As presented in today's Liturgy of the Word, the birth of Samson (cf. Jgs 13:2–7) and of Saint John the Baptist (cf. Lk 1:23–25) were the result of God's powerful intervention in the midst of human impossibility. Like the mother of Samson, Elizabeth experienced disgrace and humiliation in the society of her time due to her barrenness; but God stood by both women, and blessed them graciously by making them fruitful through the gift of a child. This demonstrates the power of God working through human impossibility. Scripture has much evidence for such a claim. God created the wonderful world from nothing (cf. Gen 1:1–2); He created human persons from the dust, and made them the crown of creation (vv. 26–28); God promised numerous descendents to Abraham even in his ripe old age (cf. Gen 12:2–4); He brought the people of Israel from their life of slavery into the promised land (cf. Ex 3:7–10); and the birth of Jesus, the Savior of the world, took place in the poverty of a stable (cf. Lk 2:10–12). All these show that nothing is impossible for God (cf. Lk 1:37). This also assures us that what is impossible for men becomes possible for those who believe in God's power.

We may be invaluable and insignificant in the eyes of others, but we are all precious and valuable in the eyes of God, Who indeed does great things for us: "Then will the eyes of the blind be opened, the ears of the deaf be cleared; then will the lame leap like a stag, then the tongue of the dumb will sing. Streams will burst forth in the desert and rivers in the steppe" (Is 35:5–6). These are the amazing signs worked by the Messiah; His marvelous intervention in human impossibility. The mothers of Samson and Saint John were righteous and blameless before God. Yet society regarded them as despised; but God made them fruitful because of their righteousness and unconditional faith in God's power, even in the midst of despair and human impossibility. Their genuine prayers and cries to God did not go to waste. Their righteousness, and their faithfulness to God, enabled them to face life with faith and optimism, despite their barrenness and hopelessness. In this grace-filled season, we are called to be on the alert for Advent virus-symptoms such as interior hope, peace, joy and love. The hearts of a great many have already been exposed to this virus, and it is possible that people everywhere could come down with it in epidemic proportions. This could pose a serious threat to all sorts of conflict in the world. The faith-stories of Elizabeth and Zachariah and the mother of Samson tell us that only those who entrust themselves to God, in deep faith, will experience the power of God's intervention, even in human impossibilities. Ask yourself: do I believe that God can lead me to accomplish great things, overcoming my human inabilities? In moments of disgrace, do I turn to God in faith, or reject Him, succumbing to humiliation and frustration?

Wisdom from St. Francis de Sales: "We must love what God loves. Now, He loves our vocation; so let us also love it, and not occupy ourselves with thinking on that of others. Let us do our duty; each one's cross is not too much for him. Do diligently the service of your vocation, and often recollect yourself, and put yourself in spirit at the feet of our Lord, and say, 'My Lord, whether I run or stay, I am all yours and you mine; whatever I do is for love of you, both this and that.' When any contradiction comes upon you, thoroughly resign yourself unto our Lord, and console yourself, knowing that His favors are only for the good or for those who put themselves in the way of becoming so" (SFS, *Thy Will Be Done,* 12-13).

Prayer: Lord God, You truly surprise me by intervening in the midst of my human impossibilities. Grant me the grace to appreciate Your many blessings in life and totally belong to You alone.

December 20th

Is 7:10–14; Lk 1:26–38

Preparation: Take a few minutes of silence, setting aside all your worries and anxieties, and become aware of the divine presence.

Listening to God's Word: "Then the angel said to her, 'Do not be afraid, Mary, for you have found favor with God. Behold, you will conceive in your womb and bear a son, and you shall name him Jesus. Mary said, 'Behold, I am the handmaid of the Lord. May it be done to me according to your word' (Lk 1:30–31, 38).

God's plan is different

We normally don't like anyone to change or alter our plans or schedules without our knowledge or without good reason. There is a story from the traditions about Saint Thomas the Apostle: Once, Jesus asked Thomas, "Are you ready to go wherever I would send you?" "Yes, Lord. I am willing to go anywhere in the world that you would send me, except to India," the Apostle replied. Jesus answered, "It is to India that I intend to send you. It is my desire that there you will preach the Gospel of God's love and become a saint." God's plan may differ from what we aspire or plan to do. To accept something that we don't like, or doing what we don't expect, is the hardest and the most challenging thing in life. When Abraham was asked by God to go to a foreign land, leaving his homeland, he followed the Lord's instruction in trust without knowing where he was going. God indeed blessed him to be the father of a great nation. So also Mary, when she was called to be the mother of the Savior, though deeply confused, surrendered to God; she trusted in His promise. Ahaz, the king of Judah, however, refused to trust in the promise of God under the pretext of not wishing to test the Lord (cf. Is 7:10–12). He was indeed proud, selfish in his motive, and fearful. He refused to trust in the promise of God that God would bring him victory, whereas Mary entrusted herself to God with a complete surrender: "I am the handmaid of the Lord. Let it be done to me according to your word" (Lk 1:38). It expresses her deep trust and total surrender to God's plan.

By her unconditional response in faith and trust, Mary made a deliberate decision to accept God's promise. Even though she faced an uncertain future as the mother of the Savior, she fulfilled her part in God's plan for human salvation. She was ready to face the challenging moments and painful situations, accepting all that would come from following God's ways. Thus she was a strong believer before becoming the mother of the Savior. Through her faith-filled response to God's call she became the new Ark of the Covenant. Saint Augustine said of Mary, "It is a greater thing for her that she was Christ's disciple than that she was His mother." The salvation history of Israel began with an act of faith by Abraham (cf. Gen 12:1–5), and the salvation history of the world began with the same act of faith by Mary. Saint John Paul II had said that "Christmas is not simply the remembrance of the Event that took place two thousand years ago when, as narrated in the Gospel, the power of God took on the frailty of a baby. It is really about a living reality that is repeated every year in the heart of believers. The mystery of the Holy Night must be lived as a spiritual event in the 'today' of the Liturgy. The Word who found a dwelling in Mary's womb comes to knock on the heart of every person with singular intensity this Christmas." God's ways are not our ways. At times we might fail to rely on God's promise of protection and guidance, making lame excuses. The way to salvation may take a sudden turn, and our plan may be scuttled unexpectedly. Jesus still calls us to be a people of faith and to trust like Mary that we will find favor with God, walking with Him in times of hardship and trials. Ask yourself: what is my attitude in such moments? Do I trust in Jesus or fall into despair? Am I ready to accept God's plan for me even if that plan is different from my expectations?

Wisdom from St. Francis de Sales: "How happy we shall be if we love this divine Goodness that has prepared such favors and blessings for us! Let us all belong to God in the midst of so much busyness brought on by the diversity of worldly things. Where could we give better witness to our fidelity than in the midst of things going wrong? Ah, solitude has its assaults, the world its busyness; in either place we must be courageous, since in either place divine help is available to those who trust in God and who humbly and gently beg for His fatherly assistance" (Marie Thibert, *Letters of Spiritual Direction,* 163).

Prayer: Gracious God, I thank You for the Incarnation of Jesus Your Son. Grant me the grace to be a person of faith, like Mary, accepting Your plan even if it is different from my expectations.

December 21st

Zeph 3:14–18; Lk 1:39–45

Preparation: Take a few minutes of silence, setting aside all your worries and anxieties, and become aware of the divine presence.

Listening to God's Word: "When Elizabeth heard Mary's greeting, the infant leaped in her womb, and Elizabeth, filled with the holy Spirit, cried out in a loud voice and said, 'Most blessed are you among women, and blessed is the fruit of your womb…Blessed are you who believed that what was spoken to you by the Lord would be fulfilled'" (Lk 1:41–42, 45).

The Visitation – a moment of shared joy

When someone whom we love visits us, or when we visit our friends and loved ones, it is truly a moment of excitement, encouragement, and affection; a grace-filled time of shared joy. This happened to Mary and Elizabeth as relatives, when they met each other with the Good News of God's blessings in their lives. After hearing about the motherhood of Elizabeth in her old age, Mary immediately traveled to visit her cousin. Taking up a challenging and hazardous journey, she came to share the joy of Elizabeth, who realized the marvelous work of God taking place in Mary. The visitation of these two mothers was the meeting of Jesus and John in the womb, and it was indeed a moment of shared joy for Mary and Elizabeth. Their visitation is the concrete expression of believers' love and care for one another, in which joy, as the central theme of salvation, is shared and proclaimed. Thus, both these mothers celebrated their faith in this visitation, rejoicing with each other, and praising God for His blessings. These two women lived in faith and trust for the rest of their lives (Lk 1:45). By their faith-sharing visitation, these two mothers played their roles perfectly well in facilitating the journey of God's Word as Good News of salvation from heaven to Mary in Nazareth by an angel, from there through Mary to Jerusalem in the house of Elizabeth and Zachariah, from Jerusalem to Galilee and Samaria in Judea by John the Baptist and Jesus, and from there to the ends of the earth through the Apostles and believers. Nothing on earth can stop this journey of God's Word bringing salvation to humanity.

As believers, we are called to be God's instruments, like Mary and Elizabeth, and to proclaim the birth of God's Word into our world; sharing the blessings of love, joy and peace with everyone. With our committed life of faith, we must make the words of the prophet Zephaniah come true: "Fear not, O Zion, be not discouraged! The Lord, your God, is in your midst, a might savior; He will rejoice over you with gladness, and renew you in his love, He will sing joyfully because of you" (Zeph 3:16–17). This is God's divine assurance for us: that every sorrow and gloom, all tragedies and difficulties, all pain and suffering, cannot continue forever. It will certainly come to an end, causing us to rejoice and celebrate God's blessings (cf. Rev 21:4). This is the purpose of Jesus' birth among us. Saint Pope John Paul II said that "the traditional Christmas tree as a very ancient custom exalts the value of life, as in winter the evergreen becomes a sign of undying life. The tree is decorated and Christmas gifts are placed under it. It reminds us of the 'tree of life' (Genesis 2:9), a representation of Christ, and God's supreme gift to humanity. The message of the Christmas tree is that life is 'ever green' if one gives, not so much material things, but of oneself, in friendship and sincere affection, fraternal help and forgiveness, in shared time and reciprocal listening." Let's not allow our weeping to be so loud as to diminish the sweet song of joy, nor our happiness to distract us from focusing our attention on the suffering of others. Ask yourself: do I increase others' joy by my visitation, or cause them pain? Do I grow, as a person of hope, by daily visiting the Lord?

Wisdom from St. Francis de Sales: "The mystery of our Lord's Nativity is also the mystery of the Visitation. Just as the most holy Virgin had to visit her cousin St. Elizabeth, we too must go very often during this octave to visit the Divine Infant lying in the manger. There we shall learn from the sovereign Pastor of the shepherds to direct, to govern and to put our flocks in order in such a way that they will be pleasing to His Goodness. The shepherds visited Him and were blessed by Him with very great joy (Lk 2:20). But St. Joseph and the most glorious Virgin received indescribably greater consolation because they assisted Him and remained in His presence. We will receive from Him an unparalleled consolation in visiting this most lovable Baby" (Visitation, *The Sermons of SFS for Advent and Christmas*, 59-60).

Prayer: Lord Jesus, thank You for visiting me as Emmanuel! Help me to experience You as "God-with-us" in my joys and sorrows so that I will share the Good News of joy to others.

December 22nd

1 Sam 1:24–28; Lk 1:46–56

Preparation: Take a few minutes of silence, setting aside all your worries and anxieties, and become aware of the divine presence.

Listening to God's Word: "And Mary said, 'My soul proclaims the greatness of the Lord; my spirit rejoices in God my savior. For he has looked upon His handmaid's lowliness; behold, from now on will all ages call me blessed. The Mighty One has done great things for me and holy is his name'" (Lk 1:46–49).

Gratitude must be our song

Praising God in gratitude is an awareness of God's saving action in our life. Though Mary is praised for her special vocation to be the Mother of the Savior (cf. Lk 1:30–31), she responds as God's servant, and her song of praise and thanksgiving is an act of faith. To a rich businessman who could not come to the realization of God's presence in his life due to his heavy schedules and business, the Master said, "As the fish perishes on dry land, so you perish when you get entangled into the world and its concerns. To survive the fish must return to the water; you must return to solitude." The businessman was aghast and said, "Should I give up all my business and go into a monastery?" "No, no. I don't say that. Hold on to your business and go into your heart. Then you will realize God's blessings in your life," (De Mello, *One Minute Wisdom,* 13). Getting entangled with the concerns of many things in the name of God does not help us to experience God in life; like the fish returning to the water for survival, it is only if we return to God with a humble and sincere heart that we will experience Him surprising us with many blessings. In the Book of Judith we read, "You are the God of the lowly, helper of the oppressed, a supporter for the weak, the protector of the forsaken, the savior of those without hope" (Jdt 9:11). Mary experienced God's goodness in her life, and expressed gratitude in her song of praise, which is a sincere worship of the heart and a joyful proclamation of God's saving actions.

As a consequence of Mary's conception by the Holy Spirit, she might have lost Joseph, her marriage, her parents, and her very life. But God intervened and Joseph took her into his home. Mary recognized with gratitude such grace-filled interventions of God in her life. In the most difficult hardships and trials, people normally complain about the silence of God; but Mary acknowledged and proclaimed God's goodness and life-saving presence (cf. Luke 1:49ff). We can notice in her song of praise how God takes the side of the poor and the lowly, defending their cause. Mary experienced such grace from God that she was overjoyed upon receiving the privilege to be the mother of the Savior, even in her lowliness. However, God humbles those who are proud and haughty in their attitudes and actions. This can happen in our life, too. We may experience only troubles and trials, or pain and suffering. We may not be able to see the hidden blessings in moments of hardship. In such situations, we must have a hope-filled attitude of faith, like Mary, believing that God still walks with us, defending our cause in those dark moments, even in our lowliness. The song of Hannah, and Mary's Magnificat, speak about the greatness of the people of faith, who experience God calling them from death to life. Their faith-response inspires us to prepare adequately for a meaningful celebration of Christmas. Ask yourself: do I blame God for my misery and lowliness, or recognize, with gratitude, the hidden blessings of God even in my troubles? How often do I praise and thank God, in faith, for blessing me in many different ways through many different people?

Wisdom from St. Francis de Sales: "You must know that to practice self-abandonment and to forsake ourselves is nothing else but to yield up and surrender our own will so that we may give it to God. We should abandon ourselves only in order that we may leave ourselves at the mercy of God's will. Many people say to our Lord, 'I give myself wholly to You without any reserve,' but very few actually practice this self-abandonment, which is nothing else but the acceptance with perfect equanimity of all the events that befall us, just as they arrive by the order of God's providence: affliction equally with consolation, sickness with health, poverty with riches, shame with glory, contempt with honor" (SFS, *The Art of Loving God*, 13-14).

Prayer: Loving Jesus, thank You for blessing humanity through Your Incarnation. Stir up my mind and heart to recognize Your blessings in life that I will always sing the joyful song of praise.

December 23rd

Mal 3:1–4, 23–24; Lk 1:57–66

Preparation: Take a few minutes of silence, setting aside all your worries and anxieties, and become aware of the divine presence.

Listening to God's Word: "So they made signs, asking his father what he wished him to be called. He asked for a tablet and wrote, 'John is his name,' and all were amazed. Immediately his mouth was opened, his tongue freed, and he spoke blessing God. All who heard these things took them to heart, saying, 'What, then, will this child be?' For surely the hand of the Lord was with him" (Lk 1:62–64, 66).

Something new is happening here!

We learn from Sacred Scripture that God's divine plan will certainly reach its fulfillment, in spite of human resistance. Sometimes God and humans may work at cross-purposes, but God's plan will finally reach its goal. Pope Benedict XVI has said that "at the beginning of a new yearly cycle, the Church sums up her proclamation to all the peoples in two words: 'God comes.' These words contain an ever new evocative power. It is not used in the past tense—God had come, nor in the future—God will come, but in the present—'God comes.' This is a continuous present, an ever-continuous action: it happened, it is happening now and it will happen again. In whichever moment, 'God comes.' The verb 'to come' says something about God's very nature. It is to simply announce God himself, that is, His being the God-who-comes." Our God comes in Jesus to do something new with us. As today's Gospel describes, the birth of Saint John the Baptist is full of miraculous signs and wonders which makes his birth an important event in salvation history. John became God's special gift to his elderly parents, removing their shame and barrenness. To everyone's amazement, his father, Zachariah, who was mute for nine months as a punishment for his disbelief, began to speak. To the surprise of his family and neighbors, he was given a new name, "John," which had never been used by anyone in his family. All those who gathered around him, recognizing that something divine was taking place, said, "What, then, will this child be?" (Lk 1:66).

Yes, God was doing something new with Saint John the Baptist. Indeed, God had sent John to prepare "the way of the Lord," for the coming of the Messiah. The prophet Malachi aptly describes the role of the messenger: "Lo, I am sending my messenger to prepare the way before me…For he is like the refiner's fire or like the fuller's lye…I will send you Elijah, the prophet, Before the day of the Lord comes…To turn the hearts of the fathers to their children, and the hearts of the children to their fathers" (Mal 3:1a, 2b, 23–24a). As an adult, John took his call to be the messenger of the Messiah very seriously, and he prepared the people of God. He influenced their thinking and inspired their faith-life by his straightforward preaching and his exemplary, ascetic lifestyle. He spoke God's word courageously, demanding from his listeners a radical change of heart. Consequently his listeners highly respected him and welcomed his preaching. He was successful in his mission as the Lord's messenger because "the hand of the Lord was with him" (Lk 1:66). The call of John, and his mission, should remind us of our own call to be messengers of God's saving intervention in our world. We must believe that whomever God calls, He also assures of His powerful and life-saving presence. As we prepare to celebrate the birth of our Savior, we must realize that God is doing something new in our life, offering us a new vision and life-purpose. Since God did something new with Saint John the Baptist, ask yourself: do I realize that Jesus has come to do something new with me, for my family and for others? Can I discern God's purpose and act on it in complete trust?

Wisdom from St. Francis de Sales: "It is the great good of our souls to be 'for God,' and the greater good to be only 'for God.' He who is only 'for God' is never sorrowful, except for having offended God; and his sorrow for that dwells in a deep but tranquil and peaceful humility and submission. Then, he raises himself up in the divine goodness, but a sweet and perfect confidence, without annoyance or bitterness. He who is 'for God' only, seeks him only; and because God is not less in adversity than prosperity, such a one remains at peace in adversity. He who is 'for God' only, often thinks of him amidst all the occupations of this life; he wishes everyone to know whom he serves, and tries to take the means proper for remaining united to him" (SFS, *Thy Will Be Done,* 241-242).

Prayer: Jesus, You are the light of our world. Help me to see something new happening because of Your birth in my life and in the world, so that I will proclaim You as the source of all blessings.

December 24th

2 Sam 7:1-5, 8b–12, 14, 16; Lk 1:67–79

Preparation: Take a few minutes of silence, setting aside all your worries and anxieties, and become aware of the divine presence.

Listening to God's Word: "Blessed be the Lord, the God of Israel, for he has visited and brought redemption to His people…to shine on those who sit in darkness and death's shadow, to guide our feet into the path of peace" (Lk 1:68, 79).

The dawn of salvation

People are so busy today with last minute preparations, and being involved with many things, as they try to get everything ready to celebrate the birth of Jesus our Savior. However, as Pope Benedict XVI has said, "Advent calls believers to become aware of the truth that God comes and they are to act accordingly. It rings out as a salutary appeal: Awaken! Remember that God comes! Not yesterday, not tomorrow, but today, now! The one true God is not a God who is there in Heaven, unconcerned with us and our history. He is the-God-who-comes. He is a Father who never stops thinking of us. As He desires to meet us, He wants to come, to dwell among us, to stay with us. His 'coming' is to free us from evil and death, from all that prevents our true happiness." This is the purpose and meaning of Jesus' Incarnation. Zachariah and Elizabeth indeed experienced the visitation of God in their lives, a visitation that reminds us to become aware of God's intervention, even in the ordinary events of our life. The Canticle of Zachariah proclaims the details of the messianic fulfillment. As a priest, Zachariah would have read in the Old Testament about God's covenant with Abraham and David (cf. 2 Sam 7:8–16). He also personally experienced the Lord's intervention in the birth of his son John (cf. Lk 1:13–20). Therefore, filled with the Holy Spirit, he realized with gratitude what the Lord had done and continues to do. This canticle is not only a prophecy of a future event, but also a song of praise for God's intervention—through Jesus—to save humanity. This song of praise by Zachariah should become our own song of hope, because Christmas is the greatest event in our human history, reminding us of God's greatest gift: salvation.

The births of Saint John the Baptist and Jesus announce God's redemption. They were born while the people of Israel suffered under dominating foreign powers: the Romans. So God was visiting the people in the midst of their oppression and suffering. The people of Israel had been longing for God's intervention, expecting Him to deliver them from foreign domination. They hoped that this powerful act of God's deliverance would be a new exodus for Israel (cf. Lk 1:71; Ps 18:77, 106:10). However, one purpose of God's redemption is not merely deliverance from political domination—though it was important for Israel—but the creation of peaceful social conditions where God's people can worship and serve God without fear and oppression, loving one another in freedom. So holiness and righteousness, as two important elements of God's covenant, are to mark the lifestyle of all believers of all ages, as a sign of being saved by God through Jesus. We know that the empty crib will be occupied by Baby Jesus on Christmas Eve. The empty crib symbolizes the absence of God in our world, and the emptiness of our life without God. Jesus, born as a Child in the crib with His arms outstretched, proclaims the message of hope: that God is in our midst. He is born among us as a little baby, inviting us to hear Him say, "I am here; I am with you always. Do not be afraid." Jesus' presence with us assures the gift of joy and the hope of new life. Ask yourself: do I come to Jesus, lying in the manger, to hear His message of hope each Christmas? Do I believe that the God who has come to save me dwells with me always, even in my struggles and troubles?

Wisdom from St. Francis de Sales: "God desired to provide a more loving gift for us who live on earth as in a desert, and who long for the joy of the Promised Land, our heavenly country. He came Himself to bring us this gift, and He came in the middle of the night. This special gift is the grace which helps us to attain what would otherwise be impossible for us; the joy and happiness of glory. Thus, in the darkness of the night our Lord was born and appeared to us as an infant lying in a manger" (Visitation, *The Sermons of SFS for Advent and Christmas,* 53).

Prayer: Loving Jesus, You are the Prince of Peace! As I celebrate today in my home Your birth among us to save humanity, help me to be a person of hope, and proclaim the message of peace.

Christmas Season - The Messiah is Around

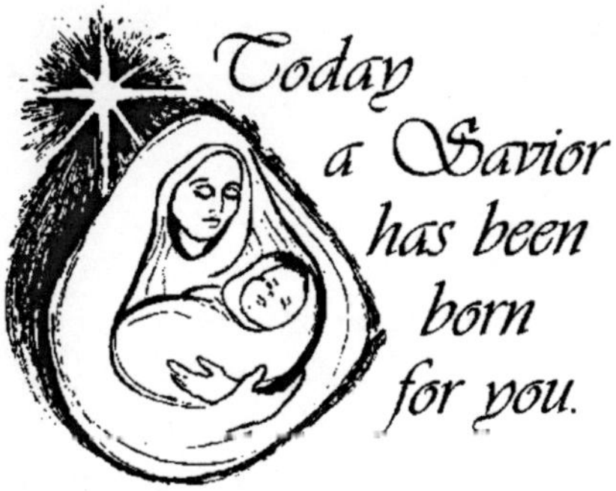

"Certainly, in the Incarnation, man divinized
And God humanized in such a way that God,
Without ceasing to be God, is man; and man,
Without ceasing to be man, is God."
(St. Francis de Sales)

December 26th - Feast of St. Stephen, the First Martyr

Acts 6:8–10, 7:54–59; Mat 10:17–22

Preparation: Take a few minutes of silence, setting aside all your worries and anxieties, and become aware of the divine presence.

Listening to God's Word: "But beware of people, for they will hand you over to courts and scourge you in their synagogues…When they hand you over, do not worry about how you are to speak or what you are to say. You will be given at that moment what you are to say…You will be hated by all because of my name, but whoever endures to the end will be saved" (Mt 10:17, 19, 22).

Enduring till the end

Martyrs are a living Gospel. Each drop of their blood is a seed of faith, sown to foster the Gospel message of Jesus and bear abundant fruit. As presented in the first reading, Saint Stephen had sown the seed of faith by shedding his blood. His martyrdom in the name of Jesus shows his faith-conviction, for he believed what he courageously preached. He knew the dangers and challenges involved, but he was determined to live by his faith, for he was filled with the Holy Spirit. Pope Francis has said that "all the people whom the Holy Spirit chooses to tell the truth to the People of God suffer persecution, and Jesus is precisely the model, the icon. The Lord took upon Himself all the persecutions of His people. This history of persecution is the way of the Lord: it is the path of those who follow the Lord…this story ends as always in the Resurrection, though only by passing by way of the Cross." In the Gospel, Jesus warns the disciples to be aware of the challenges and hardships they will face in life because of Him. Yet Jesus assured the disciples of His continued power and grace working through them, which would guide them through all such ordeals. By courageously facing his death, and generously forgiving his executioners as did Jesus his Master, Saint Stephen proved himself a faithful disciple. He was one of the first deacons ordained by the Apostles to take care of the material needs of the Christian community. Full of grace and fortitude, he performed great wonders and signs among the people in the name of Jesus. He spoke with such wisdom and eloquence that his hearers were unable to resist him (cf. Acts 6:8–10). So the elders of a certain synagogue in Jerusalem plotted against him, and accused him of blasphemy. Consequently the whole assembly became enraged at Stephen and stoned him (vv. 12–14, 7:57–58).

Whether it is an act of mob violence, or a pre-planned judicial execution of religious authorities, the insane act of killing human persons in the name of God is an outrageous act continued to be carried out even in our day. However, Saint Stephen's martyrdom is an inspiration for believers to live by uncompromising faith, always honoring and promoting human freedom and dignity. As Jesus warned the disciples, God's children will face opposition, rejection, hardship, trials and suffering, in many different forms, even in their own living situations. They will be hated by all, even, perhaps, by friends and loved ones (cf. Mt 10:17–18). Though such experiences may be life-threatening, leading us to despair, we must be aware of the Lord's promise to provide us with the necessary wisdom and courage to face all such terrible situations in our hostile world (vv. 19–20). If we cling to Jesus in trust and total surrender, He will enable us to endure until the end. Saint Stephen is a model for such enduring faith. He professed his faith courageously, spoke the truth about Jesus fearlessly, and faced a violent death. He confidently fixed his eyes on God, praying for those who killed him (cf. Acts 7:60). Ask yourself: do I face challenges or persecutions, whether great or small, in the same spirit as Saint Stephen, with my eyes fixed on Jesus? Do I speak the truth courageously without compromise?

Wisdom from St. Francis de Sales: "Blessed will they be who pronounce [the name of Jesus] reverently and with a most profound appreciation of our Savior having ransomed us with His blood and by His passion. Those who call upon the name well at the time of death will be saved. The opposite will be the fate of those who do not speak it well and who pronounce it tepidly and without fervor" (Visitation, *The Sermons of SFS for Advent and Christmas,* 101).

Prayer: Jesus my Savior, thank You for the gift of Saint Stephen, who lived for You even to the point of facing death. Enable me to remain faithful to You, enduring until the end as Your witness.

December 27th - Feast of St. John the Apostle

1 Jn 1:1–4; Jn 20:1a, 2–8

Preparation: Take a few minutes of silence, setting aside all your worries and anxieties, and become aware of the divine presence.

Listening to God's Word: "So Peter and the other disciple went out and came to the tomb. They both ran, but the other disciple ran faster than Peter and arrived at the tomb first; he bent down and saw the burial cloths there, but did not go in...Then the other disciple also went in, the one who had arrived at the tomb first, and he saw and believed" (Jn 20:3–5, 8).

Believing without seeing

After the death and resurrection of Jesus, Saint John, one of the twelve Apostles, was believed to have lived in Ephesus for over one hundred years. It is said that his only slogan throughout his life was, "Little children, love one another." His life witness and teachings were the foundation of all the writings attributed to him. Saint John writes, "The way we came to know love was that he laid down his life for us; so we ought to lay down our lives for our brothers" (1 Jn 3:16). Traditionally, the Gospel of Saint John, three letters, and the Book of Revelation, are all attributed to him. In all his teachings, whatever Saint John proclaims about Jesus has come from his personal experience of the Master. So it is said that "he saw and believed" (Jn 20:8). The spiritual Master always insisted to his disciples that what he taught was nothing; what he did was nothing. The disciples gradually discovered the meaning of the Master's saying: that wisdom comes to those who learn nothing and unlearn everything, because the Master said, "Transformation is the consequence of not something done or accomplished but of something dropped; that is, self-emptiness." Through his experience with Jesus, both during His ministry and by witnessing to His death and Resurrection, Saint John the Apostle reached the state of self-emptiness; he became a humble instrument, leading others to Jesus.

Saint John's teachings about Jesus highlight two things. First, his experience with Jesus in history is so profound that he says with conviction,

"What we have heard, what we have seen with our eyes, what we looked upon and touched with our hands concerns the Word of life; we proclaim now to you" (1 Jn 1:1, 3). This is indeed a life-enriching and life-transforming experience, and a courageous proclamation of his deep faith in Jesus. Secondly, what he believed, he proclaimed by his life of faithful witness. He had heard the teachings of Jesus, witnessed to His miracles, and saw Him dying on the Cross in humiliation. The Apostle was transformed by all these experiences with Jesus; he firmly believed in what he saw at Jesus' tomb, and he proclaimed courageously and convincingly what he believed. The Apostle lived the rest of his life witnessing to the history of human salvation through Jesus, Who came to live with us in order to save us from sin, offering us eternal life. Saint John's teachings summarize the whole Gospel teaching of Jesus: "God is love, and whoever remains in love remains in God and God in him" (1 Jn 4:16). Hence, the Apostle's faithful witness helps us to go through the process of self-emptiness, firmly believing that Jesus is our Savior, Who died for love of us, that through this faith, we may have life eternal (cf. Jn 20:31). "It is by the path of love, which is charity, that God draws near to man and man to God. But where charity is not found, God cannot dwell. If, then, we possess charity, we possess God, for God is Charity" (Saint Albert the Great). Saint John did not see, touch or hear Jesus in the tomb. Along with Saint Peter, he saw the empty tomb and believed in the mystery of Jesus' resurrection. Ask yourself: do I experience the life-giving presence of Jesus in my life? Do I see the light of the risen Jesus in moments of emptiness and darkness?

Wisdom from St. Francis de Sales: "Total commitment never to abandon God or to forsake his gentle love serves as a counterweight to our spirits, to preserve them in holy equanimity in the midst of all the changing circumstances which the conditions of this life bring to them. Bees, when caught in a storm in the fields, take up little stones to keep their balance in the air and not to be easily carried away by the storm. Similarly, we hold on eagerly to the precious love of God by our firm determination. Thus we remain steadfast in the midst of the inconstancy and instability of consolations and afflictions, whether temporal or spiritual, exterior or interior" (SFS, *IDL, Part IV,* Ch. 13, 319-320).

Prayer: Jesus my Savior, Your Apostle Saint John faithfully witnessed to Your death and resurrection. Guide me with Your Spirit, that I may experience Your love and be Your witness throughout my life.

December 28th - Feast of the Holy Innocents

1 Jn 1:5–2:2; Mt 2:13–18

Preparation: Take a few minutes of silence, setting aside all your worries and anxieties, and become aware of the divine presence.

Listening to God's Word: "When they had departed, behold, the angel of the Lord appeared to Joseph in a dream and said, 'Rise, take the child and his mother, flee to Egypt, and stay there until I tell you. Herod is going to search for the child to destroy him.'…When Herod realized that he had been deceived by the magi, he became furious. He ordered the massacre of all the boys in Bethlehem and its vicinity two years old and under, in accordance with the time he had ascertained from the magi" (Mt 2:13, 16).

The value of human life

Our human history up to our present day bears evidence that innocent people unjustly suffer at the hands of tyrants and dictators. Governments, trying to exterminate the opposition, oppress and slaughter their own innocent people. Religious fundamentalists do not hesitate to kill innocent people, including children and elders, in the name of God and religion. In all such events, innocent children become the most vulnerable people, suffering violence and death. Whatever be the reason given for such ruthless acts of murder, the root cause of all such horrible deaths of innocent people is an attitude of inhumanness, selfishness, and hatred. At the birth of Jesus, too, the innocent male children suffered an unjust death because of Herod's selfishness and greed for power. Herod was afraid of losing his political power, and so he feared the rise of another king who would challenge his claim to the throne. In his effort to destroy the rival king at his birth, he killed innocent male children (cf. Mt 2:16) and they became the first martyrs in the name of Jesus, the Savior of the world. What message does this incident convey to us? First, the birth of the Messiah amidst the evils of our inhuman world explains the true purpose of Jesus: that as Savior, He has come to redeem humanity from sin and evil, replacing the culture of death with a culture of life. Secondly, in spite of human tyranny and hurdles, God's plan will fulfill its purpose. Therefore, following the direction of the angel, Joseph and Mary saved the baby Jesus and helped fulfill the divine plan for human salvation (cf. Mt 2:13). While rejoicing at the birth of our Savior, we should discern and follow the direction of God, overcoming all our fears.

We must also learn to respect and honor human persons, especially the innocent ones, as God's precious gifts, defending their life and freedom to live honorably. Today we need to listen to the teaching of the Apostle Saint John: "But if we walk in the light as he is in the light, then we have fellowship with one another, and the blood of his Son Jesus cleanses us from all sin" (1 Jn 1:7). Let this teaching of the Apostle become an inspiration for us in our faith-journey, to walk always in the light of Jesus like the Holy Innocents, who were the first martyrs in His name. "Let us therefore give ourselves to God with a great desire to begin to live thus, and beg Him to destroy in us all traces of sin, and to establish His life within us" (Saint John Eudes). Our own tears, and the cries and tears of innocent people, will be as real as those of Rachel in the Old Testament. Not only our own sins, but also the wrong actions and injustices of others, will cause us tears and sorrows. However, the feast of the Holy Innocents reminds us that all suffering and sorrow will produce not only tears and weeping; but a blossoming into wonderful new life. The cries of innocent people will always find their reward in Jesus, Who is the source of all hope. Ask yourself: do I understand Jesus' self-gift in the Incarnation, and shine like a little lamp in my dark world? Can I respect others' dignity, and foster fraternal solidarity in my faith-community and in my family?

Wisdom from St. Francis de Sales: "Let us practice well holy resignation and pure love of our Lord. To love God in sugar—little children would do as much. But to love Him in wormwood, that is the test of our amorous fidelity. To say *Vive Jesus* (live Jesus) on the mountain of Tabor, St. Peter, while still carnal, has courage enough; but to say *Vive Jesus* on Mount Calvary—this belongs only to the Mother, and to the beloved disciple who was left to her as her son. So behold, I commend you to God to obtain for you that sacred patience. He would fashion your heart in total accordance with His will in order to lodge and reign therein eternally. Whether He does it with hammer, or with the chisel, or with the brush, it is for Him to act in accordance to His pleasure" (SFS, *Thy Will Be Done,* 99-100).

Prayer: Jesus my Savior, You are the source of my hope for new life. Help me to overcome my tears, fears and sorrows, and shine like a little lamp in difficult times, always honoring human life.

December 29th - Within the Christmas Octave

1 Jn 2:3–11; Lk 2:22–35

Preparation: Take a few minutes of silence, setting aside all your worries and anxieties, and become aware of the divine presence.

Listening to God's Word: "When the days were completed for their purification according to the law of Moses, they took him up to Jerusalem to present him to the Lord…The child's father and mother were amazed at what was said about him; and Simeon blessed them and said to Mary his mother, 'Behold, this child is destined for the fall and rise of many in Israel, and to be a sign that will be contradicted'" (Lk 2:22, 33–34).

The model family

In our modern world, we normally regard a family in which there is peace, happiness, success, and prosperity, as a model family. People naturally expect a certain standard of living and an honorable status from such families in order to be an inspiration. In this sense, the Holy Family may not fulfill the criteria of a model family as we expect it today, because the family of Joseph and Mary seemed to be stormed by struggles and suffering, trials and hurdles, poverty and failures. The marriage of Joseph and Mary began with confusion and anxiety (cf. Mt 1:18–20). They became homeless at Bethlehem, and Mary had to give birth to her first child in a stable (cf. Lk 2:6–7). They faced threats to the Child's life (cf. Mt 1:13), and they had to flee to Egypt and live there as refugees (cf. Mt 2:14–15). They lived in Nazareth, hiding after returning from Egypt (cf. Mt 2:23). At the presentation of the Child Jesus in the temple, the words of Simeon troubled them and caused anxiety (cf. Lk 2:34–35). One might wonder how such a family, experiencing such problems and hardships, can be a model family. However, the Holy Family is a model family because of the way Joseph and Mary weathered those stormy moments of life to find meaning and happiness. In all such events and experiences, they loved each other dearly, and banded together in faithfulness, building up a family of love, loyalty, and trust in God's promise. We hear from Saint John who says in his first letter that whoever claims union with Jesus must live as He lived, in faithfulness to the Father, showing love and compassion to all people (cf. 1 Jn 2:6). Joseph and Mary lived a life of such loving commitment to each other at every moment. They learned and discerned from all their experiences to grow in faith, and they obeyed God's will.

As Saint John explains, "Whoever loves his brother remains in the light, and there is nothing in him to cause a fall" (cf. 1 Jn 2:10). We too must ground our faith-life on genuine love for each other, in our families and communities, if we want to live in the light of Jesus. Love is the reason God came down in Jesus to be among us. Love is the cause of Jesus' self-abasement for human salvation. Love must be the ground of our faith-life as followers of Jesus. Without true love and fraternal solidarity, our faith-communities and families will be shattered. Henry Nouwen says, "When I choose to let go of my sometimes petty and superficial wishes and trust that my life is precious and meaningful in the eyes of God, something really new, something beyond my own expectations begins to happen for me. To wait with openness and trust is an enormously radical attitude toward life. It is giving up control over our future and letting God define our life. It is living with the conviction that God molds us in love, holds us in tenderness, and moves us away from the sources of our fear" (James E. Adams, *Living Hope*, 17). Saint Joseph and the Virgin Mary chose to trust in God and lived in hope. Ask yourself: following their model, do I grow in love and band together with my brothers and sisters, living with optimism? How do I see God guiding me to create in my family a happy atmosphere to live in fraternal love?

Wisdom from St. Francis de Sales: "Most important is that you don't lose heart, be patient, wait, do all you can to develop a spirit of compassion. I have no doubt that God is holding you by the hand; if He allows you to stumble, it is only to let you know that if He were not holding your hand, you would fall. This is how He gets you to take a tighter hold of His hand. Be completely, absolutely, irrevocably His" (Marie Thibert, *Letters of Spiritual Direction*, 158).

Prayer: God my loving Father, thank You for the gift of the Holy Family as a model and inspiration. Grant me Your grace to live in hope, and follow Your plan for me in faithfulness.

December 30th - Within the Christmas Octave

1 Jn 2:12–17; Lk 2:36–40

Preparation: Take a few minutes of silence, setting aside all your worries and anxieties, and become aware of the divine presence.

Listening to God's Word: "There was also a prophetess, Anna, the daughter of Phanuel, of the tribe of Asher. She was advanced in years, having lived seven years with her husband after her marriage. She never left the temple, but worshiped night and day with fasting and prayer. And coming forward at that very time, she gave thanks to God and spoke about the child to all who were awaiting the redemption of Jerusalem" (Lk 2:36–38).

People of gratitude

Celebrating special events for the children in our families is a gracious moment of jubilation and blessings for the whole family. Love grows deeper, relationships are strengthened, and new friendships are forged at the words of blessing spoken about the children. This is our human experience. This happened to Jesus upon his presentation in the temple by his parents, surrounded by people of faithfulness and gratitude. Saint Joseph and the Virgin Mary, as persons of righteousness and gratitude, fulfilled the requirements of the law in celebrating the birth of Jesus, the Savior of the world, and recognized the fulfillment of God's promises in their life. The ritual of presenting Jesus in the temple expresses their deepest awareness of God at work in their lives, and their religious faith-commitment. They lived within the covenantal community, and they now introduced Jesus into that community of faith. There were also people like Simeon and Anna, who as people of devotion and trust in God's promises, represent the pious ones of Israel, who learned to praise God in everything, faithfully awaiting the fulfillment of God's promises. All of them recognized and experienced God's presence and blessings in the ordinary events of their lives. As Anna was committed to God's service from a young age, she represents the pious widows of both Judaism and the early Church. John proclaims that "the world and its enticement are passing away. But whoever does the will of God remains forever" (1 Jn 2:17). This was true of Anna the prophetess.

Though as a widow, Anna experienced humiliation in the society of her time and went through discouraging moments in life; yet, she remained loyal to her religious faith-traditions, without yielding to the enticement of worldly concerns. By her life of prayer and her attitude of gratefulness to God, she learned to be a person of optimism, faithfully following the will of God, and hoping for the fulfillment of God's promise of redemption. Jesus grew up among such people of true faith and gratitude. Therefore, Saint Luke writes, "The child grew and became strong, filled with wisdom and the favor of God was upon him" (Lk 2:40). It is said that "you must develop an attitude of gratitude, and give thanks for everything that happens to you, knowing that every step forward is a step toward achieving something bigger and better than your current situation" (Brian Tracy). In our faith journey, we might certainly experience the enticement of our world. It might come in the form of being captivated by the outward appearance of things, of pretentiousness, of surrendering to the glamorous and the glittering, or as love for the gadget-civilization of this world that can misdirect our purpose or distract us from following God's will. On such occasions, we must learn from people like Saint Joseph and the Virgin Mary, from Simeon and Anna, to deepen our awareness of God's presence and blessings even in the ordinary events and difficult times of our life. Ask yourself: how do I learn to be a person of optimism and gratefulness? Do I give in to the enticement of the world, or with determination and steadfastness discern and follow God's will?

Wisdom from St. Francis de Sales: "We must consider that there is no vocation that has not its irksome aspects, its bitterness, and disgusts. And what is more, except for those who are fully resigned to the will of God, each one would willingly change his condition for that of others: those who are bishops would like not to be; those who are married would like not to be, and those who are not married would like to be. Whence comes this general disquietude of souls? But whoever is not fully resigned let him turn himself here or there, he will never have rest. A person who has not the fever of self-will is satisfied with everything, provided that God is served. We must not only will to do the will of God, but in order to be devout, we must do it joyfully" (SFS, *Thy Will Be Done*, 9-10).

Prayer: Thank You, Jesus, for revealing God's love by Your Incarnation. Guide me to face my daily life-realities in the light of faith and hope that I may be committed to follow Your will.

December 31st - Within the Christmas Octave

1 Jn 2:18–21; Jn 1:1–18

Preparation: Take a few minutes of silence, setting aside all your worries and anxieties, and become aware of the divine presence.

Listening to God's Word: "In the beginning was the Word, and the Word was with God, and the Word was God. He came to what was his own, but his own people did not accept him. And the Word became flesh and made his dwelling among us, and we saw his glory, and the glory as of the Father's only Son, full of grace and truth" (Jn 1:1, 11, 14).

God's solidarity

Living with dear ones in a closely-bonded relationship as a family is the most profound experience of love, happiness, and blessing that gives meaning to our human existence. The Gospel today reminds us that Jesus has brought us greater happiness and meaning for our life through His Incarnation. In the Gospel according to Saint John, we do not find the infancy narrative of Jesus, as the other evangelists (Matthew and Luke) have presented. Rather Saint John begins the Gospel with a beautiful hymn that describes the eternal existence of Jesus with the Father as God: "In the beginning was the Word, and the Word was with God, and the Word was God" (Jn 1:1). Though this hymn explains the divine existence of Jesus before all time, what is said in v. 14 is the important historical event which manifested God's intervention in our human history: "And the Word became flesh and made his dwelling among us." "Dwelling among us" means that God actually pitched His tent among us. The eternal God became Emmanuel, and chose to live among us. Thus, Jesus, Who is God Himself, took our human nature so as to be in solidarity with us in our sufferings and struggles, our fortunes and misfortunes, our successes and failures. It is not that we deserve Jesus' solidarity with us; but because He loves us so much, He has come to share our lives, adopting us as "children of God" and making us people of freedom (vv. 12–13). This is the greatest Good News; it is encouraging and hope-giving for us.

In this divine solidarity with humanity, Jesus' Incarnation fulfilled the Old Testament promise of the Messiah's divine protection. By coming among us, Jesus revealed the Father's love and grace in abundance and granted us life in its fullness (cf. Jn 3:16; 10:10). The disciple once asked the Master, "Why is it that everyone here is happy and joyful except me?" "Because they have learned to see goodness and beauty everywhere and in everyone," said the Master. "Why don't I see the same goodness and beauty everywhere and in everyone?" "Because you cannot see and experience outside of you what you fail to see inside of you," the Master said. Jesus, as the Incarnation of a loving and merciful God, shared love and compassion, grace and blessings, with everyone—welcoming all people as God's dear children. We, too, are called to live in love and fellowship by following the way of Jesus and bring the blessings of God's love to others through a life of fraternal solidarity. Our faith-life determines our identity as children of a merciful God. Therefore, we cannot be unbelieving, by denying or by teaching falsely, like the Antichrists (cf. 1 Jn 2:18–19, 22), the truth about God's revelation in the Incarnation of Jesus. Let us understand that as God's children, we must become channels of God's grace for others. As God's solidarity with us in Jesus assures God's nearness in our life, our personal presence with others will be the greatest gift that would enrich their life. Ask yourself: while celebrating the divine solidarity of Jesus with us through His Incarnation, do I find fraternal solidarity with others as belonging to God's human family? Do I respect and honor the poor and the lowly, sharing God's blessings and offering them the Good News of hope for new life?

Wisdom from St. Francis de Sales: "'Whether we live or whether we die,' says the Apostle, 'if we belong to God, who shall separate us from the love and charity of God?' No, nothing shall ever separate us from this love, neither trials nor anguish, neither death nor life, neither present sorrow nor fear of future troubles, not the wiles of evil spirits, neither the height of consolation nor the depth of affliction, neither consolation nor dryness must ever separate us from that holy charity which is rooted in Jesus Christ" (Marie Thibert, *Golden Counsels of SFS,* 11-12).

Prayer: Lord Jesus, thank You for finding solidarity with me by Your Incarnation. Grant me Your grace, that I might show fraternal love to people around me, appreciating their goodness.

January 2nd - The Christmas Season

1 Jn 2:22–28; Jn 1:19–28

Preparation: Take a few minutes of silence, setting aside all your worries and anxieties, and become aware of the divine presence.

Listening to God's Word: "And this is the testimony of John. When the Jews from Jerusalem sent priests and Levites to him to ask him, 'Who are you?' he admitted and did not deny it, but admitted, 'I am not the Messiah.' So they asked him, 'What are you then? Are you Elijah?' And he said, 'I am not.' 'Are you the Prophet?' He answered, 'No.' So they said to him, 'Who are you, so we can give an answer to those who sent us? What do you have to say for yourself?'" (Jn 1:19–22).

Who am I?

It is said that "self-knowledge includes awareness of our strengths as well as our weaknesses. When we can accept that both pluses and minuses often come wrapped up in the same package, we can stop being so hard on ourselves and start working with what we have" (Earnie Larsen and Carole Hegarty, *Believing in Myself*, July 25). Each one of us can come to such self-knowledge by asking the question, "Who am I?" In the Gospel narrative today, the priests and the Levites asked John the Baptist, "Who are you?" By this question, the religious leaders demanded to be told by Saint John the Baptist whether he was a prophet like Elijah, or the long-expected Messiah himself. John, in his reply, chose not to prove his personal glory and credentials (his credentials being his authority and privilege to preach and baptize) but instead confessed his mission, saying, "I am 'the voice of one crying out in the desert, make straight the way of the Lord…'" (Jn 1:23). This clearly points out that his prophetic mission as the forerunner of the Messiah proved his identity as a prophet. He was aware of the purpose of his call, and of the responsibility and commitment involved, including his vulnerability as he prepared the people for the Messiah's coming. John realized that his worthiness consisted in recognizing his unworthiness to touch the sandal of the Messiah (v. 27). His confession of his prophetic mission reveals not his own personal glorification, but his self-effacement, by which he focused on the person of Jesus rather than on his own self-affirmation and self-proclamation.

Our self-knowledge about our true identity and life-commitments will direct us on the right path to make good decisions, and to do positive things in life. Lack of genuine self-knowledge and our life-purpose will land us in the wrong place, making poor choices. Saint John, in his first letter, instructs us that not the one who denies, but the one who confesses Jesus, the Son, has the Father (cf. 1 Jn 2:23). If the teachings of Jesus remain in us, we will remain in the Son and the Father, experiencing the gift of eternal life (vv. 24–25). The purpose of our life as God's children is to remain constantly in loving communion with God, overcoming temptations to faithlessness. As we celebrate the presence of the Baby Jesus in our midst, reflecting on the prophetic role of Saint John the Baptist, let us ask ourselves who we are as individual persons, with our own goodness and shortcomings; our gifts and talents; our responsibilities and faith-commitments as believers. Such self-awareness will help us to play our different roles for the betterment of our community and society. There is an Indian saying that "Our wisdom results from critical questions; our happiness is the consequence of pain and suffering." Hence, though it may be hard and painful, can I ask the question "Who am I?", so that I can grow in faith, and understand my own blessings and shortcomings? Do I project and proclaim my own credentials, or learn to value the importance of others' goodness? How do I understand God's actions in my life to find true happiness?

Wisdom from St. Francis de Sales: "When asked, 'Who are you?' do not be content to answer like little children in catechism class, 'I am a Christian,' rather live in such a manner that one will recognize clearly in you a person who loves God with his whole heart, one who keeps the commandments, frequents the sacraments, and does all things worthy of a true Christian. I do not mean that when we are asked who we are we must not say that we are Christians. Oh, certainly not! It is the most beautiful title we can give ourselves. All I mean is that it is not enough to be called a Christian if we do not perform the works of a Christian" (Visitation, *The Sermons of SFS for Advent and Christmas,* 10-11).

Prayer: God of love and goodness, thank You for creating me with uniqueness. Help me to be aware of my gifts and my weaknesses, so that I will learn to affirm and value the uniqueness of others.

January 3rd - The Christmas Season

1 Jn 2:29-3:6; Jn 1:29–34

Preparation: Take a few minutes of silence, setting aside all your worries and anxieties, and become aware of the divine presence.

Listening to God's Word: "The next day he saw Jesus coming toward him and said, 'Behold, the Lamb of God, who takes away the sin of the world.'… I did not know him, but the one who sent me to baptize with water told me, 'On whomever you see the Spirit come down and remain, he is the one who will baptize with the holy Spirit.' Now I have seen and testified that he is the Son of God" (Jn 1:29, 33–34).

The Lamb of God

We know from our experiences that a testimony is proof for establishing or rejecting the truth about someone or something. As we heard in the Gospel narrative today, Saint John the Baptist, as the forerunner of the Messiah, testified about Jesus' identity and mission, saying, "Behold, the Lamb of God, who takes away the sin of the world" (Jn 1:29). A few verses later he announces, "Now I have seen and testified that he is the Son of God" (v. 34). This testimony of Saint John affirms that Jesus is the Lamb of God; that He will baptize with the Holy Spirit; and that He is the Son of God. By this declaration, inspired by the Holy Spirit, Saint John announced Jesus' identity of pre-existence as the Son of God, Who became our Messiah, living among us through His Incarnation. Saint John also proclaimed, to the people gathered around him, the mission of Jesus: that He has become the Lamb of God (through His self-sacrifice) to redeem us from sin and death. The people's hope of redemption lies in recognizing and believing in Jesus as the Son of God. The prophets of the Old Testament anticipated that the Spirit would reside in the Messiah, who would bring renewal and transformation to the lives of God's people (cf. Is 11:1–2, 42:1, 61:1–3). In the light of this understanding, Jesus is presented as the one who will baptize people with the Holy Spirit, as a sign of new creation, and with the promise of new life. Thus, Saint John, by his personal witness to the truth about Jesus' identity and mission, led the people to believe and to follow Him as the long-awaited Messiah.

The title "Lamb of God" applied to Jesus from the mouth of Saint John the Baptist is to be understood in the Old Testament imagery of the suffering servant. In Isaiah, we read about God's servant suffering for the sins of the people (cf. Is 53:7), and about the Passover lamb, sacrificed for the deliverance of Israel from their life of slavery in Egypt (cf. Ex 12:1–13). Though in Judaism the Passover lamb was not viewed as a sacrifice for people's sins, it was by this symbolism that the early Church understood Jesus as the Passover Lamb, and interpreted His death on the Cross, in the light of the Eucharist, as a sacrifice for the sins of the world (cf. 1 Cor 5:7–8). Thus, the metaphor "Lamb of God," referring to Jesus, explains His mission as the Redeemer of the world from its sinfulness (collective brokenness) by His self-sacrifice (cf. the Book of Revelation, chapter 5, where Jesus is depicted as a victorious Lamb). This personal testimony of Saint John is a wake-up call to all believers, to be the Lord's witnesses in our own life situations. All our liturgical celebrations, and all our preaching about our newborn Savior, must lead us to have a better understanding and personal experience of Him as the One Who has redeemed us by His self-gift, saving us from the powers of sin and death, and restoring us as God's children (cf. 1 Jn 3:1). Saint John the Apostle says, "If you consider that he is righteous, you also know that everyone who acts in righteousness is begotten by him" (1 Jn 2:29). Ask yourself: do I have a right understanding of Jesus' self-sacrifice for my sins? Am I interested in merely fulfilling the ritual requirements of my faith, or in becoming a true witness of Jesus, as was Saint John?

Wisdom from St. Francis de Sales: "Do not look forward to the mishaps of this life with anxiety, but await them with perfect confidence so that when they do occur, God, to whom you belong, will deliver you from them. He has kept you up to the present; and He will help you in all situations. When you cannot walk, He will carry you. Do not think about what will happen tomorrow, for the same eternal Father who takes care of you today will look out for you tomorrow and always. Either He will keep you from evil or He will give you invincible courage to endure it" (Marie Thibert, *Golden Counsels of SFS*).

Prayer: Lord Jesus, Saint John the Baptist gave up everything to be Your witness. Help me, by Your grace, to grasp the true meaning of Your self-emptiness, that my faith witness may inspire others to follow You.

January 4th - The Christmas Season

1 Jn 3:7–10; Jn 1:35–42

Preparation: Take a few minutes of silence, setting aside all your worries and anxieties, and become aware of the divine presence.

Listening to God's Word: "The two disciples heard what he said and followed Jesus. Jesus turned and saw them following him and said to them, 'What are you looking for?' They said to him, 'Rabbi' (which translated means Teacher), 'where are you staying?' He said to them, 'Come, and you will see.' So they went and saw where he was staying, and they stayed with him that day" (Jn 1:37–39).

Come and see

Our personal experience as a witness will be a powerful inspiration and motivation for others to make the right decision, or pursue the right direction in life. Once, a salt doll journeyed thousands of miles over land until it finally came to the sea. It was fascinated by this strange moving mass of water which it had never seen before. "Who are you?" said the salt doll to the sea. The sea smilingly replied, "Come in and see." So the doll waded in. The farther it walked into the sea the more it dissolved until there was only a very little of it left. Before that last bit dissolved, the salt doll exclaimed joyfully in wonder, "Now I know what I am." (De Mello, *Song of the Bird*, 98). The disciples of Saint John the Baptist were inspired by their teacher's personal witness to Jesus and followed Him. This episode of the first disciples following Jesus exemplifies the master-disciple relationship. The more their relationship with Jesus developed, the more committed they became as disciples in following Him. When John's disciples followed Jesus, He asked them, "What are you looking for?" (Jn 1:38). These first words of Jesus convey one of the central questions in this Gospel. What do people desire, or seek, in following Jesus? It is a profound question of inner-seeking to find a purpose-driven life. As a reply, the disciples said to him, "Rabbi…where are you staying?" and Jesus said to them, "Come, and you will see" (vv. 38b–39a). It is a personal invitation which Jesus offered to the disciples: to see and discover with the eyes of faith, for themselves, Who Jesus is; that they might have a better understanding of His identity and mission.

This dialogical encounter shows that the disciples had an inner thirst for God, and so they became seekers of meaning and truth in life. Understanding their earnest desire for God, Jesus invited them: "'Come, and you will see.'…and they stayed with him that day" (v. 39b). This was their profound personal encounter with, and experience of, Jesus. "Staying" emphasizes the disciples' personal relationship with Jesus, which changed the whole purpose and direction of their lives. From then on, they became disciples and daring missionaries. This "come and see" experience of the disciples was a crucial moment for them, as it was a moment of enlightenment and inner awakening; a grace-filled moment of decision-making and life-commitment. From their personal experience, they in turn became evangelizers, announcing to their companions their experience of finding the Messiah (vv. 40–42). Saint John the Apostle, in his first letter, teaches, "The person who acts in righteousness is righteous, just as he is righteous" (1 Jn 3:7). As God is our loving Father, we are introduced into God's human family by Jesus, the Son of God. Therefore, we are to live a righteous life, avoiding all that is evil, and developing a profound personal relationship with Jesus and others as a believing community. Like the first disciples, we must be seekers of God in our life. Ask yourself: do I foster an inner longing to have a "come and see" experience with Jesus in my life? Do I seek and find Jesus in all that I do, and in everything that happens to me?

Wisdom from St. Francis de Sales: "In all you have to do, rely wholly on God's providence through which your plans will succeed. Nevertheless, strive quietly on your part to cooperate with God's designs. Imitate little children who with one hand hold fast to their father while with the other they gather strawberries or blackberries from the hedges. So too if you gather and manage the goods of this world with one hand, you must always hold fast to your heavenly Father's hand and turn toward Him from time to time to see if your actions and occupations are pleasing to Him" (Marie Thibert, *Golden Councils of SFS,* 23).

Prayer: Thank You, Jesus, for the grace to be Your disciple. Lead me by Your Spirit to have a personal relationship with You, like the first disciples, that I may follow You in faithfulness.

January 5th - The Christmas Season

1 Jn 3:11–21; Jn 1:43–51

Preparation: Take a few minutes of silence, setting aside all your worries and anxieties, and become aware of the divine presence.

Listening to God's Word: "The next day he decided to go to Galilee, and he found Philip. And Jesus said to him, 'Follow me.'... Philip found Nathanael and told him, 'We have found the one about whom Moses wrote in the law, and also the prophets, Jesus, son of Joseph, from Nazareth.' But Nathanael said to him, 'Can anything good come from Nazareth?' Philip said to him, 'Come and see'" (Jn 1:43, 45–46).

Evangelization

Our common human experiences tell us that shared blessings are multiplied, and shared sorrows disappear quickly. Today's Liturgy of the Word highlights how people are able to discern their call to discipleship by sharing with others their faith-experiences. Once, four men went through a forest and suddenly they came to a highly elevated wall. They became curious to know what would be on the other side of this huge wall. So they made a ladder and the first one climbed the ladder to see. Seeing the natural beauty behind the wall, the man exclaimed, "Oh! What a great sight! It is an awesome, amazing and heavenly beauty," and he came down with excitement. The second and the third also reacted in the same way. They wondered at the beautiful sight but did not tell others what they had found. The fourth one also climbed the ladder, and wondered at the natural beauty; but went home and shared his experience with others, leading them to experience the amazing beauty of nature. As today's Gospel presents, Philip, to his surprise, encountered Jesus, Who invited him to join Him, saying, "Follow me" (Jn 1:43). By sharing his experience of Jesus with others, he led them to encounter Him. According to John's theological approach, "following" is a metaphor for discipleship that describes the transformed state of life which the disciples received because of their encounter with Jesus.

By following Jesus, the Light, the disciples will not walk in darkness but will have the light of life (cf. Jn 8:12). As a good shepherd, Jesus will walk ahead of the disciples (the sheep), and they will follow Him, recognizing His voice (cf. 10:4, 27). Accordingly, after following Jesus and experiencing Him personally, Philip shared his experience of Jesus with Nathanael, saying, "We have found the one about whom Moses wrote in the law, Jesus, the son of Joseph, from Nazareth" (Jn 1:44). Nathanael's natural response was, "Can anything good come out of Nazareth?" (v. 46). This reveals the ordinariness, the simplicity, and littleness of Nazareth. Nathanael could not believe that anything good could be found in the ordinariness of Nazareth. However, he experienced, to his surprise, that Jesus recognized him and called him to discipleship; and Nathanael confessed his faith, saying, "Rabbi, you are the Son of God; you are the king of Israel" (v. 49). If we take an optimistic and positive approach, we can encounter Jesus even in the ordinary events of life, discovering the richness of God's blessings in abundance. By our faith-witness, we can inspire and motivate others to experience Jesus; whereas by taking a negative approach, we fail to be good "finders." Saint John, in his first letter, instructs us, "Children, let us love not in word or speech but in deed and truth" (1 Jn 3:18). By dying for us on the Cross, Jesus showed us the depth of His love for us (v. 16). By sharing love and showing compassion for our brothers and sisters, we can become evangelizers for others, so that they can experience Jesus in their lives. Ask yourself: do I devalue the goodness of others because of their ordinariness and littleness? Am I an optimist or a pessimist in my approach? How can I inspire others by my faith-witness?

Wisdom from St. Francis de Sales: "Who knows that the unhappy soul will be converted? The greatest sinners often become the greatest penitents, as we see in the case of David. And who are we that we should judge our brother [or sister]? Were it not for the grace of God we should perhaps do worse than he [or she]. This life is our pilgrim way, in which those who now stand may fall, and those who have fallen may, by grace, be set on their feet again. We must certainly entertain sentiments of boundless confidence in the goodness of God, who is infinite in mercy to those who invoke Him. Jesus Christ even offered His peace, His love and His salvation to His disciple Judas who betrayed Him with a kiss. Why, then, may He not have offered the same favor to the unhappy sinner? Is the arm of God shortened?" (Pierre Camus, *The Spirit of St. Francis de Sales,* 79).

Prayer: Jesus my Savior, Your birth assures me that God has not abandoned me. Help me to follow You without guile, so that by my faith-witness, I will lead others to find new life in You.

January 6th - The Christmas Season

(The following is used if Epiphany is celebrated on January 7th or January 8th)

1 Jn 5:5–13; Lk 3:23–38 (or Mk 1:7–11)

Preparation: Take a few minutes of silence, setting aside all your worries and anxieties, and become aware of the divine presence.

Listening to God's Word: "When Jesus began his ministry he was about thirty years of age. He was the son, as was thought, of Joseph, the son of Heli, the son of Matthat, the son of Levi…the son of Enos, the son of Seth, the son of Adam, the son of God" (Lk 3:23–24, 38).

My faith identity

Every one of us is very much interested in reconstructing our family tree, because establishing our family ancestry and our distant relatives serves as an important social need for us. It enlightens us regarding our age-old family traditions, the importance of people involved in building our family, and their hard work and sacrifices in fostering our family values. In the Old Testament, we can find frequent genealogies (about twenty-five of them) which fulfill an important social function. In those days, recording genealogies, especially among royal and priestly families, was important for succession and kingship, conferring power and privileges. In the New Testament, we can find only two genealogies, which are in the Gospels of Saint Matthew and Saint Luke; and both are concerned with Jesus' ancestry. While Matthew features the genealogy beginning from Abraham through David to Joseph, the foster-father of Jesus, Luke presents the genealogy in the reversal order, beginning with Jesus, through Joseph, and ending with Adam, the "son" of God. This clearly explains the author's theological motive. By connecting Jesus with Adam, the "son" of God, Luke emphasizes that Jesus is the Son of God. The angel announced Jesus, before His birth, as the Son of God (cf. Lk 1:30–32). In the temple, Jesus, at His young age, gave indication of His divine Sonship (cf. Lk 2:48–49). At His baptism in the River Jordan, the heavenly voice declared, "You are my beloved Son" (Lk 3:22; Mk 1:11). Now through the genealogy, described before the beginning of His ministry, Luke shows how Jesus is truly the Son of God. Immediately after presenting the ancestry of Jesus, Luke shows, in the temptation story, how Satan challenged Jesus' identity as the Son of God (cf. Lk 4:1–13).

Jesus always proved His identity as God's Son by His faithfulness to God the Father, even in the midst of temptations and struggles. Moreover, by connecting Jesus with Adam, Luke emphasizes the universal character of God's salvation. The significance of Jesus' identity as Son of God and Savior of Humanity is not only for the descendents of Abraham, but for all the descendents of Adam, and for all the nations of the earth, as mentioned in Luke 3:6: "All flesh will see the salvation that comes from God." Thus, the evangelist affirms the identity of Jesus before His ministry. The rest of the Gospel narratives, regarding His teachings and actions, including His death and Resurrection, show how Jesus lived up to that identity. As Saint John explains, it is through the Son, Jesus, that God gave us eternal life, and we are called to possess Jesus and live by Him (cf. 1 Jn 5:11–12). While reflecting on the genealogy of Jesus, we must understand that it connects Jesus with God, with Israel, and with humanity. The same Jesus has become human, like us, through His Incarnation; and standing within the history of God's covenant with Israel, Jesus entered our human history, declaring the dawn of God's reign, to call together a new community of people. Following Jesus' model, we must live up to our identity as true followers of Jesus and faithful children of God the Father, even in our daily struggles, miseries and misfortunes. Ask yourself: do I feel proud of my faith, or do I compromise it for my convenience? How do I prove my identity as a child of God?

Wisdom from St. Francis de Sales: "It is necessary that those who live among worldly people and embrace true devotion join together in a holy and sacred friendship. By such means, they encourage, assist and support themselves well. Just as those who walk on level ground do not need a helping hand, but those who are on a dangerous and slippery path support one another to walk more safely, so too those who are religious do not need particular friendships. But those who are in the world do need them, to save themselves and help one another, in the midst of so many difficult paths they have to cross" (SFS, *IDL, Part III,* Ch. 19, 223-224).

Prayer: Gracious God, I thank You for adopting me as Your beloved child. Guide me with Your Spirit to prove my identity by faithfully discerning and fulfilling Your divine plan in my life.

January 7th - The Christmas Season

(The following is used if Epiphany is celebrated on January 8th)

1 Jn 5:14–21; Jn 2:1–11

Preparation: Take a few minutes of silence, setting aside all your worries and anxieties, and become aware of the divine presence.

Listening to God's Word: "On the third day there was a wedding in Cana in Galilee, and the mother of Jesus was there. Jesus and his disciples were also invited to the wedding. When the wine ran short, the mother of Jesus said to him, 'They have no wine.' (And) Jesus said to her, 'Woman, how does your concern affect me? My hour has not yet come.' His mother said to the servers, 'Do whatever he tells you'" (Jn 2:1–5).

Hope-giving initiative

If someone comes to our aid when we are lost on our way, or if our friends and neighbors support us in the most difficult times, encouraging and assisting us, we feel as though we experience God, standing just in front of us. We could never forget such grace-filled moments, and we will be ever-grateful to all such people coming into our life. As the Gospel narrative presents today, the Virgin Mary and Jesus came to the rescue of the family hosting the marriage banquet. When the wine ran out, the family was in great trouble, facing social dishonor and humiliation. Mary, aware of the family's problem, came to Jesus with an implied request to do something in order to help the family in trouble (cf. Jn 2:3–5); and at the request of His mother, He did change the water into wine, and saved the family from social humiliation (cf. 2:7–9). However, let us focus here on the importance of Mary's initiative, and the meaning of Jesus' action. Among those attending the marriage, at least some of them would have been aware of the problem the family faced. Yet only Mary, without any request from the family or anyone else, took the initiative to help the family, and save them from disgrace. This is indeed a hope-giving initiative by Mary, reaching out to others in great need. Her action of timely help, and of bringing hope to those in despair, proved her to be a person of faith and hope.

This is the message of hope which Saint John, in his first letter, offers us: that Jesus, the Son of God, if we ask Him anything—in faith and trust—according to His will, we must believe that He listens to us and hears our prayers (cf. 1 Jn 5:13–14). Mary lived by such faith in God that her very life stands as a model for all believers to be persons of hope. Jesus, too, by changing the water into wine, brought hope to the family in trouble, and enlightened the disciples with the promise of hope. The superabundance of wine which Jesus offered is a sign of Messianic hope. It is believed that in the Old Testament the abundance of good wine was an eschatological symbol of joy upon the arrival of a new age (cf. Amos 9:13–14; Joel 2:18). Jesus' act of changing water into wine at the beginning of His ministry is the fulfillment of the Old Testament eschatological hopes, and the inaugural act of God's salvation. We, too, may come across people in dire need who are faced with great troubles and hardships. Jesus calls us to be of some help to such people, offering them hope and encouragement, that they might experience God's blessings even in the darkest moments. Being with Jesus at "the hour" of His glorification at Cana (cf. Jn 2:3–5, 7–9), and again at the Cross (cf. Jn 12:32; 19:25), Mary continues her hope-giving initiative of interceding for us before God. Ask yourself: do I seek God's guidance, and never give up my hope-giving initiatives? Can I act as an instrument of hope for others?

Wisdom from St. Francis de Sales: "We have always to undertake the long and arduous struggle between fear and hope, always believing that hope is strong and will always come out victorious, because we know and believe in the infinite power of God who is always ready to come to our rescue (*XVII,* 161)." "Fear and hope go together. If fear does not go together with hope, it is no longer fear but only despair; and hope without fear is mere presumption. You have, then, to fill the valleys of fear made deep with the consciousness of your grave imperfections and sins; you have to fill them with a confidence that is mingled with the fear of God" (SFS, *Conf. IX,* 443, from *The Art of Utilizing Our Faults,* 60, 61).

Prayer: Mother Mary, thank you for inspiring me with your faith life. Intercede for me, so that following your faith-example, I will reach out to others through my hope-giving initiatives.

The Epiphany of the Lord - All are Included

"Let us come close to the crib. If you love riches,
You will find the gold that the kings brought;
If you are looking for the smoke of honors,
You will find that in the incense; and if you take
Delight in the delicacies of the senses, you will find
The delicate perfume of myrrh pervading the stable."
(St. Francis de Sales)

(The following days are celebrated between Epiphany and the Baptism of Jesus)

Monday after Epiphany, or January 7th

1 Jn 3:22, 4:6; Mt 4:12–17, 23–25

Preparation: Take a few minutes of silence, setting aside all your worries and anxieties, and become aware of the divine presence.

Listening to God's Word: "'The people who sat in darkness have seen a great light, on those dwelling in a land overshadowed by death, light has arisen.' From that time on, Jesus began to preach and say, 'Repent, for the kingdom of heaven is at hand.' He went around all of Galilee, teaching in their synagogues, proclaiming the Gospel of the kingdom, and curing every disease and illness among the people" (Mt 4:16–17, 23).

Light shining in darkness

If we want to understand the real motive of God's reign among us, and grasp the deeper meaning of Jesus' teachings, we must understand the relevance of certain places; the significance of the socio-political-religious context of the time; and the nature of people's living conditions. As highlighted in the Gospel account today, Jesus' Galilean ministry in Capernaum, as well as the regions of Zebulun and Naphtali; and the people whom Jesus cured, restoring their wholeness of health, provide the living context for understanding Jesus the Messiah, Who has come as a light into the darkness. Jesus' moving into Galilee was seen as a courageous undertaking in His mission. Galilee, in the first century, consisting of a half-Gentile population, half-pagan in cult and bilingual in language, became the local arena of Jesus' public ministry. Capernaum was an important trade centre of the time but had a bad reputation, because of its multiculturalism and paganism. It was the least Jewish of the Judaic towns. The Old Testament tribes of Zepulun and Naphtali suffered very badly during the devastating aftermath of Assyrian invasion and suppression in 732 B.C. The mention of these different places and various cultures, as well as people's socio-economic situation, indicate their detestable living conditions.

In this context, the saving activity of Jesus, the Messiah, began in these unexpected places and among these despised people, rather than in the religious capital of Jerusalem or in the desert, which was a place of spiritual discernment. The prophecy of Isaiah quoted in the Gospel of Saint Matthew (4:16), says that "the people who sit in darkness have seen a great light, on those dwelling in a land overshadowed by death light has arisen"; this offered a renewed hope to the oppressed people under the Assyrian domination. With the coming of Jesus and His preaching about the nearness of God's reign as the basis and object of Christian hope, the prophecy of Isaiah had been fulfilled in Jesus (cf. Mt 4:14–16; Is 8:23, 9:1). His arrival was seen as a light bringing comfort and consolation, and offering a new orientation for the suffering and despised people. When we face struggles, trials and hardships in life, or while going through discouraging moments of failure, becoming humiliated and despised, we should not fall into discouragement. We might be stormed by low self-esteem and the thought that everything is lost, and feel doomed forever. It is in such situations that Jesus comes as a light, offering us the message of encouragement, solace, and renewed hope for better possibilities of a bright future. Saint John reminds us that whatever happens to us, we should believe in Jesus Christ, and keep loving one another; that we must continue to remain in Him and He in us (cf. 1 Jn 3:23–24). Ask yourself: do I create life situations in which people are despised and humiliated, or do I offer them opportunities to rise up from their fallen state and lowliness? Can I welcome Jesus into my life despite my failures, and follow His light?

Wisdom from St. Francis de Sales: "This life is short but is very valuable, for by means of it we are able to acquire eternal life. Happy are those who know how to use it for this purpose and how to apply these passing moments to gain a happy eternity. Nothing is so pleasing to the heart of God than to see us persevering in the exercise of small virtues. It is just these very virtues that can make us perfect if we persevere in them to the end, rather than the big virtues that we can exercise only from time to time" (SFS, *Letters, 1997*, from *Every Day with SFS*, 338).

Prayer: Jesus my Light, You proclaimed the dawn of God's reign for human liberation. Grant me Your grace, to shine as Your light and lead people to believe in the hope of new possibilities.

Tuesday after Epiphany, or January 8th

1 Jn 4:7–10; Mk 6:34–44

Preparation: Take a few minutes of silence, setting aside all your worries and anxieties, and become aware of the divine presence.

Listening to God's Word: "By now it was already late and his disciples approached him and said, 'This is a deserted place and it is already very late. Dismiss them so that they can go to the surrounding farms and villages and buy themselves something to eat.' He said to them in reply, 'Give them some food yourselves'" (Mk 6:35–37).

Being compassionate

It is disheartening to see, in one part of the world, many people suffering from acute poverty and dying of hunger; while in other parts of the world, people living in affluence waste a lot of food. As we heard in the Gospel narrative today, Jesus, realizing that His listeners had been with Him for a long time, did not wish to send them away hungry. Saint Mark touchingly describes the reaction of Jesus, saying, "When he disembarked and saw the vast crowd, his heart was moved with pity for them, for they were like sheep without a shepherd" (Mk 6:34). Here, Jesus recognized the spiritual thirst and the physical hunger of the people. Therefore, He taught them many things and also fed them with the minimum food available: two fishes and five barley loaves (cf. Mk 6:34c, 41–42). It is a sign of blessings in superabundance, created by God's compassionate love. When loving compassion is shared and practiced, miracles happen, and God's blessings come forth in abundance (cf. vv. 42–43). Once, God decided to visit the earth, and so He sent an angel to take a survey of the people's living situation prior to His visit. The angel, after some time, came back and reported, "I found most of the people on earth lacking food, employment, healing from illness, and they are badly in need of the message of comfort and encouragement." God said, "Then I shall incarnate in the form of food for the hungry, work for the unemployed, give the grace of healing for the sick, and offer words of encouragement for the discouraged." By His acts of compassion, Jesus had validated His teaching about God the Father as One Who was loving and compassionate. Jesus experienced God as a loving Father, and that is what He revealed in His actions, showing compassion for the poor, the hungry, and the destitute around Him.

Saint John teaches in his first letter that "God sent his only Son into the world so that we might have life through him" (1 Jn 4:9). Transmitting life to everyone is the nature of Jesus, as the Messiah, and that was the purpose of His coming into our world. The manner in which Jesus gives life to all who believe in Him is through love and compassion, fulfilling people's spiritual and physical needs, especially those who are excluded as being poor, hungry, and sinful. Thus, Jesus is portrayed as the image of a loving God, Who cared for the people of Israel in the wilderness by providing for their needs (cf. Ex 16:4–15); and as a compassionate shepherd who feeds his flock in abundance (cf. Ez 34:11–16). The virtue of compassion means to feel as one with those who suffer. So, the Apostle teaches us that it is "not that we have loved God, but that he loved us and sent his Son as expiation for our sins" (1 Jn 4:10). This is the nature of God's loving compassion, demonstrated by Jesus toward humanity. An act of compassion is the concrete expression of true love, and by this love, we come to know and experience God in life. The Talmud says, "When man shows compassion for others, God will show compassion for him." Therefore, where there is love, there is God; where there is God, there is peace, joy, and fulfillment of human aspirations. Ask yourself: do I live in love and share love with others? How do I express my compassion and mercy for others, to help human persons become fully alive?

Wisdom from St. Francis de Sales: "Live in peace and joy. Our Lord looks at you with so much love and compassion; and the weaker you are, the more His love for you grows warm and tender. Never harbor thoughts, which would go in the reverse direction. If these thoughts come and pester you, pay no heed to them; turn your mind away from them and cling to God with a humility that is bold and courageous. Speak to Him about His sacred and indescribable goodness which pours itself out on us, loving our small and weak, poor and abject nature, despite all its infirmities" (SFS, *Conf. XVIII,* 171, from *The Art of Utilizing Our Faults,* 135-136).

Prayer: Lord, Jesus, You revealed God the Father by Your acts of compassion. Grant me the grace, to be compassionate toward others, and experience the nearness of God's reign.

Wednesday after Epiphany, or January 9th

1 Jn 4:11–18; Mk 6:45–52

Preparation: Take a few minutes of silence, setting aside all your worries and anxieties, and become aware of the divine presence.

Listening to God's Word: "When it was evening, the boat was far out on the sea and he was alone on shore. Then he saw that they were tossed about while rowing, for the wind was against them. About the fourth watch of the night, he came toward them walking on the sea. But when they saw him walking on the sea, they thought it was a ghost and cried out. They had all seen and were terrified. But at once he spoke with them, 'Take courage, it is I, do not be afraid!'" (Mk 6:47–50).

God's personal name

The Gospel narrative today, about Jesus walking on the sea, reveals the marvelous manifestation of His divine identity in controlling the natural powers, and His life-giving presence in the most serious conflicts and crises of people's lives. The sea, in the Old Testament, connotes both the source of life (cf. Gen 1:10, 20; Ps 23:2) and a symbol of destructive power (cf. Ps 18:16; 69:1–2; Is 57:20). Yet God's power is expressed in the control of water (cf. Gen 1:2, 6–9; 8:1–3; Job 26:5), and His saving power is manifested in the great events of bringing the people through the waters of the Red Sea (cf. Ex 14:21–28; Is 43:16) and of the River Jordan (cf. Josh 3:13–16; 4:18–23). All such references portray how God controls and triumphs over the cosmic powers that threaten human life. The sea-rescue epiphany of Jesus portrays the fear-filled drama of the utter darkness and crises of human life through the images of the powerful waves, and by the cries of the frightened disciples. In this situation of crisis and chaos, Jesus is seen bringing order and calm to the sea, and saving the lives of the disciples by His life-giving presence: the divine "I AM." So He said, "Be courageous; it is I, do not be afraid" (Mk 6:50). This divine "I AM," as the formula of divine self-revelation, signifies God's personal name and His saving presence among His people (cf. Ex 3:14; Is 41:4; 43:10–11). God acts according to the nature of His being, and His promise as a loving and compassionate God Who is in complete control of the whole of creation.

Such a God is present through Jesus in the lives of people, particularly in their most difficult moments of trials and crises.

We, too, face life-situations or events which cause us discouragement and despair, as well as anxieties and fears for survival; we experience moments of darkness and confusion, not knowing what to do or where to go. We become frightened and lose hope. We struggle to find a way out of such problems and terrifying situations. In the face of such challenging moments in our faith-life, we even, at times, question the relevance of faith in Jesus; and cry out desperately with an attitude of hardheartedness and disbelief as to why God has deserted us. However, in all such life-threatening situations, we must believe in the life-saving presence and assurance of Jesus telling us: "Be courageous; do not be afraid for I am here with you." The Apostle teaches us that if we acknowledge that Jesus is the Son of God and live by this faith, God remains in us and we are in God (cf. 1 Jn 4:15–16). As the saying goes, "Perfect love casts off fear." As long as we are determined to love Jesus and believe in His grace-filled presence, we will fear no more, but have only hope and courage in Him alone. There is nothing in our faith-journey that we must be frightened of. Let us understand this wisdom: "Fear less, hope more; eat less, chew more; whine less, breathe more; talk less, say more; hate less, love more" (Unknown). Ask yourself: do I believe in the promise of Jesus Who assures me of His divine protection? Like the disciples, do I cry out to Jesus, seeking in trust and hope for His wisdom and guidance in fear-filled and confusing moments?

Wisdom from St. Francis de Sales: "The holy mother Church wants us to ponder deeply on the grandeur of the mystery of the most holy Nativity of our Lord. To do this, let us first humble our understanding, realizing that we are totally incapable of exhausting the great depth of this uniquely Christian mystery as only Christianity has, in Jesus, ever fathomed how God is man and man is God. Christians have been more enlightened and have had the honor of knowing the Incarnation, that man is God and God is man although even they are incapable of completely penetrating its mystery" (Visitation, *The Sermons of SFS for Advent and Christmas,* 51-52).

Prayer: Lord Jesus, thank You for strengthening me in my fears. Guide me to experience You in my life, so that I may trust in Your divine protection, and live in hope, finding refuge in You alone.

Thursday after Epiphany, or January 10th

1 Jn 4:19-5:4; Lk 4:14–22

Preparation: Take a few minutes of silence, setting aside all your worries and anxieties, and become aware of the divine presence.

Listening to God's Word: "He unrolled the scroll and found the passage where it was written: 'The Spirit of the Lord is upon me, because he has anointed me to bring glad tidings to the poor. He has sent me to proclaim liberty to captives and recovery of sight to the blind, to let the oppressed go free, and to proclaim a year acceptable to the Lord'" (Lk 4:17–19).

Human liberation – God's mission

The Sabbath service of the Jewish people of Jesus' day consisted of the Shema prayer, the recitation of the Decalogue, the eighteen benedictions, the reading of the Scriptures including the Psalms, the exposition, and a blessing. However, the choice of a passage from the prophetical writings was left to the Reader. Every male Israelite had the right to perform this reading and offer an explanation. Jesus, as a pious Jew, made use of this right, reading from the Book of Isaiah, which describes clearly His mission program. After experiencing His union with the Father and understanding the demands of His vocation by prayer and fasting in the desert, Jesus began His ministry with a well-defined paradigmatic mission-program (cf. Lk 4:18–19). As today's Gospel narrative presents, the beginning Jesus made was a beginning amongst a people of faithlessness, hardheartedness and rejection (cf. vv. 22–24), yet He began His ministry with optimism and trust in God, Whom He experienced as a loving Father. In every society, the poor, the captives, the blind, and the oppressed, are vulnerable and outcast people: impoverished, neglected, and excluded from human fellowship. Jesus had deliberately chosen such people as the focus of His mission. In this light, Isaiah's prophecy (cf. Is 61:1–2) defines the personal identity of Jesus, the kind of Messiah He would be, and the nature of His ministry.

Once, the students asked their novice master, "What does living in Christian authenticity mean?" He said, "To be a Christian is not to know the answers to all the questions but to begin to live according to the voice of one's inner self where the question is born." He was speaking of an attitude of inner listening, of awareness of God's presence, and of openness to the divine mystery. To demonstrate the nearness of God and help the people experience His loving care, Jesus had compassion on such people who were struggling to survive. Therefore, their liberation became the ultimate goal of His mission. By this proclamation, Jesus announced that He is not a political figure concerned about the national deliverance of a particular people. Rather, He is a prophetic Messiah proclaiming God's promise of liberation for all people, regardless of nationality, gender, race, region, church, or group. Therefore, Jesus' proclamation affirms the radical inclusiveness of God's grace, offering total human liberation to everyone. All believers can be instruments of such grace-filled new life and no human limitation can curtail it. Jesus faithfully fulfilled this mission of human liberation without compromising it, even in the face of death. As believers, to ignore the cries, the sorrows, the pains, and the needs of people around us, is to ignore the meaning of Jesus' presence among us, rejecting His Incarnation. Therefore, if we boast of loving God unreservedly while refusing to love our brothers and sisters, we prove ourselves to be liars, because we cannot truly love God whom we don't see if we fail to love our neighbors whom we can see (cf. 1 Jn 4:20–21). Therefore, as a Spirit-filled faith-community following the radical path of Jesus, we must orient all our actions toward winning human liberation—not excluding people from our fellowship. Ask yourself: do I welcome people and reach out to them in fraternal love or discriminate against them?

Wisdom from St. Francis de Sales: "Let us be what we are and let us be it well to do honor to the Master whose work we are. People laughed at the painter who wishing to represent a horse, painted a perfect bull. The work was fine in itself, but of little credit to the workman, who had another design, and had done well by chance. Let us be what God likes so long as we are His, and let us not be what we want to be, if it is against His intention. For if we were the most excellent creatures under heaven, what would it profit us if we were not according to the pleasure of God's will? Rejoice in our Lord and keep your heart in peace" (SFS, *Thy Will Be Done,* 20).

Prayer: Gracious God, thank You for redeeming me through Jesus Your Son. Grant me the grace to follow His radical way of listening to the cries of others without discrimination.

Friday after Epiphany, or January 11th

1 Jn 5:5–13; Lk 5:12–16

Preparation: Take a few minutes of silence, setting all your worries and anxieties, and become aware of the divine presence.

Listening to God's Word: "Now there was a man full of leprosy in one of the towns where he was; and when he saw Jesus, he fell prostrate, pleaded with him, and said, 'Lord, if you wish, you can make me clean.' Jesus stretched out his hand, touched him, and said, 'I do will it. Be made clean.' And the leprosy left him immediately" (Lk 5:12–13).

Humanness – symbol of God's blessings

One of the most influential gestures that attracted people to Jesus was the gesture of humanness. We read in the Gospels that Jesus sat with the lowly, ate with the sinners and outcasts, praised the poor, touched the sick, and wept with the afflicted. All such gestures are signs of love and compassion, acceptance and solidarity, respect and honor. As the Gospel account today shows, after calling the first disciples by promising them, "You will be catching men" (cf. Lk 5:10), Jesus touched a leper and healed him. Through this miracle, Jesus taught the disciples that the manner of gathering people for God's kingdom of love and compassion is through gestures of humanness and fraternal solidarity with those afflicted and excluded from the communal fellowship. Those who were affected by leprosy were thoroughly ostracized at the time of Jesus. Such people were regarded as a menace to society and family honor. However, Jesus, through His gesture of humanness, showed His power to break through the social prohibitions to welcome and save such outcast people. The afflicted man's request indicates the wretchedness of his living condition, and the power of his faith in Jesus to heal him. The response of Jesus to the suffering man shows that He did not stand at a distance like other people, fearing contamination or defilement. Rather, He touched the leper with love and compassion (v. 13) revealing God's solidarity with marginalized people. By disregarding the ceremonial taboo of touching unclean people like the lepers, Jesus manifested the nature of His compassionate acts, to break through the natural fear and aversion in coming into contact with such people.

Indeed, Jesus became defiled in the eyes of the society, to make the defiled people honorable and lovable. Through the loving gesture of human touch, Jesus radicalized the concrete demonstration of God's love for humanity in healing, forgiving, and restoring people to newness of life. The Apostle proclaims that God has given us eternal life in Jesus Christ; and whoever possesses the Son has life in total freedom and happiness (cf. 1 Jn 5:11–12). Jesus teaches us, the believing community today, that we should not bring disgrace to people by our acts of exclusion and rejection due to their suffering, weakness, misery, or socio-economic status. Rather it is in these conditions of life that we must love and care for them, treating them with love, honor, and humanness. Let us think about the following Christmas gift suggestions: "A firm handshake to a shaky soul, a kind word to a lonely person, a warm smile to the disheartened, a sincere concern for someone troubled, a feeling of compassion for the neglected, a comforting thought for the bereaved, a respect for the dignity of others, a sincere effort to defend the rights of individuals, a word of encouragement to help a seeking soul, and a joy-filled Merry Christmas wish to all" (Unknown). By His compassionate touch, as a sign of humanness, Jesus removed the people's social stigma of lowliness and exclusion from others, and fulfilled the demands of His programmatic mission proclaimed at Nazareth. Ask yourself: following Jesus' model of human approach, do I treat others with honor, dignity and humanness, or exclude them in disrespect?

Wisdom from St. Francis de Sales: "God loves with intensely tender love those of us who are happy enough to abandon ourselves entirely to His fatherly care, letting ourselves be governed by His divine providence without wasting time by considering if the effects of this providence will be useful, profitable, or harmful for us. We can be assured that from all that has been sent to us from His fatherly and lovable heart, God will draw goodness and value, provided that we have placed all our confidence in Him and that we say willingly, 'I place my spirit—my soul, my body, and all that I am—into your blessed hands' to do with me as you wish" (Marie Thibert, *Golden Counsels of SFS*).

Prayer: Lord Jesus, You treated everyone with love, dignity and humanness. Heal me of my pride and selfishness, so that I may treat others with compassion, honor, and respect.

Saturday after Epiphany, or January 12th

1 Jn 5:14–21; Jn 3:22–30

Preparation: Take a few minutes of silence, setting aside all your worries and anxieties, and become aware of the divine presence.

Listening to God's Word: "So they came to John and said to him, 'Rabbi, the one who was with you across the Jordan, to whom you testified, here he is baptizing and everyone is coming to him.' John answered and said, 'No one can receive anything except what has been given him from heaven. You yourselves can testify that I said (that) I am not the Messiah, but that I was sent before him. So this joy of mine has been made complete. He must increase; I must decrease'" (Jn 3:26–30).

Honest appreciation

Sometimes there would be a rush of visitors making a violent noise so that the silence of the monastery was shattered. This greatly disturbed the disciples, making them upset because they were not able to concentrate on their meditation and prayer, but the Master was undisturbed by all this and seemed to be just as content and happy with the noise as with the silence. To the disturbed and protesting disciples, the Master said one day, "Silence is not the absence of sound, but the absence of self" (De Mello, *One Minute Wisdom*, 126). Saint John had such an attitude of self-abasement, for he was undisturbed by opposition, accusations, complaints or compliments. He became so completely free of his self-aspirations and demands that he took his call seriously and lived by it. According to the Jewish wedding custom, the friend of the bridegroom occupies an important position, taking care of all the nuptial arrangements and accompanying the groom until the moment he takes possession of his bride. Yet the friend is only a secondary figure; the groom is the important person. Drawing an explicit lesson from the marriage custom of the time (cf. Jn 3:28), Saint John the Baptist expressed his delight at the great success of Jesus. For John, Jesus' successful ministry was not an occasion for complaint or sadness but a reason for rejoicing (v. 29a). Therefore, realizing the importance and the centrality of Jesus and His ministry to redeem the world, John joyfully proclaimed, "He must increase; I must decrease" (v. 30).

From the very beginning, John testified that Jesus was greater than him (cf. Jn 1:27, 30). John is not the light; Jesus is the Light (1:8–9). Accordingly, John demonstrated openness to, and delight in, Jesus' successful ministry, although it meant that John's ministry would soon come to an end. John's acceptance of his role as a messenger, revealing Jesus to the new Israel, reminds believers that the success of the Gospel must take precedence over the self-glorification of one's personal effort and achievement. Learning from John's witness, we must acknowledge and appreciate the giftedness and goodness of others in our communities and families, even as it is found in little ways. We should not even hesitate to keep aside our self-acclamation, but recognize and encourage others in their success. It is true that we all might fail in this area. Even virtuous people can be easily entrapped by the insidious human tendency to jealousy, bitter controversy, and theological hairsplitting, to the point of fighting against one another. It is self-defeating if we do not properly use our given opportunities to help and enable others to do their best. We cannot make others shine in life without first making ourselves shine. Jesus has come to give us a spirit of discernment to know the truth (cf. 1 Jn 5:20–21). Therefore, let us lose no opportunity to stand up in order to appreciate and encourage one another. Ask yourself: do I celebrate the success of my faith-witness as a sign of the success of the Gospel? Am I generous in affirming and appreciating the goodness and talents of others?

Wisdom from St. Francis de Sales: "The great secret of continuing faithfully in the way of holiness is to be very humble. Be humble and God will always be with you and will appreciate your good will. Ask Him humbly and sincerely that if till now you have not served Him faithfully and well, that He deign to forgive you and to strengthen you in your resolution to detach yourself from all earthly things and to abandon yourself entirely into His arms and to serve Him faithfully till the end. We should never be troubled whenever we commit some fault, for often the Holy Spirit is more lavish with His gifts with people who give themselves to Him in love and affection" (SFS, *Conf. XIX,* 211, from *The Art of Utilizing Our Faults,* 157-158).

Prayer: Lord Jesus, thank You for guiding me even in the dark moments of life. Grant me the grace of wisdom to seek Your goodness in others and learn to appreciate their giftedness.

Sundays and Feast Days - Staying Awake

"Be watchful! Be alert!
You do not know when the time will come...
May he not come suddenly and find you
Sleeping."
(Mk 13:33, 36)

First Sunday of Advent, Year A

Is 2:1–5; Rom 13:11–14; Mt 24:37–44

Preparation: Take a few minutes of silence, setting aside all your worries and anxieties, and become aware of the divine presence.

Listening to God's Word: "Therefore, stay awake! For you do not know on which day your Lord will come. Be sure of this: if the master of the house had known the hour of night when the thief was coming, he would have stayed awake and not let his house be broken into. So too, you also must be prepared, for at an hour you do not expect, the Son of Man will come" (Mt 24:42–44).

The future is already in the present

Visitation and preparation, invitation and expectation, are everyday life experiences. We invite someone and we anxiously expect that person's coming. When someone visits us, we are well-prepared, and earnestly wait for that person. At the beginning of the Advent season, the Liturgy of the Word emphasizes the need for watchfulness and ever-preparedness for the Lord's coming, by reminding us to live our present life meaningfully. This holy season reminds us that the Lord's future, glorious coming is already implied in His present day visitations. Saint Bernard speaks about three comings of Jesus: in His first coming, Jesus took on the human form, and lived among His people. His second coming will be in glory and majesty. His coming in the in-between-time is in spirit and power. Inspired by His first coming, and encouraged by His second coming to live in hopeful expectation, we, as disciples of Jesus, are to be aware of His daily coming into our life. It involves an attitude of readiness and prayerfulness, that we will have the strength to withstand challenges and tribulations, and stand blameless before the Lord. Furthermore, we must know that the meaning of Christmas determines the importance of the Advent season. If Christmas has little value for us, then Advent means nothing except a routine change into another liturgical season. If Christmas is about the reception of the great gift of God's salvation in Jesus (cf. Rom 13:11), then Advent becomes an important season of watchfulness and readiness. In this light, Advent is rightly understood to be a season of heightened awareness and inner-awakening.

As a grace-filled season, Advent enables us to evaluate our faith-response to God's unconditional love in Jesus. It involves the spiritual journey of examining our attitudes and approaches toward life and toward people, as we renew our relationship with God and with one another. This inner-awakening will prompt us to rise above our daily cares and concerns, anxieties and worries; to take a fresh look at our life of faith with its peaks and valleys, promises and disappointments. As Isaiah says, by our life of heightened awareness and watchfulness we will be able to follow the way of the Lord and make concrete decisions to walk in His light (cf. Is 2:3, 5), joyfully welcoming Jesus' daily involvement in our present life. As Paul instructs, it is time to wake up from sleep and cast off the works of darkness, putting on the armor of light (cf. Rom 13:11–12). This is not the armor that creates violence, conflict, disharmony, despair, and death, but the armor of Jesus Christ, Who came among us as the light of the world (cf. Jn 1:3, 8:12), establishing peace, offering joy, ensuring justice, and creating unity and solidarity among people, and thus transmitting life to everyone. We cannot remain passive, expecting Jesus' future coming with a time-table that we are uncertain about. He might surprise us with His sudden and unexpected coming. Until then, we must stay awake, by fulfilling our daily faith-commitments and building bridges between people to overcome hatred and disharmony. Ask yourself: during this holy season, am I ready to recognize the presence of Jesus in my families and faith communities? Do I put on the armor of light, or the armor of darkness?

Wisdom from St. Francis de Sales: "In order to journey steadily, we must apply ourselves to doing well the stretch of road immediately before us on the first day of the journey, and not waste time wanting to do the last lap of the way while we still have to make it through the first. Remember this well: we are sometimes so busy being good angels that we neglect to be good men and women. Our imperfections are going to accompany us to the grave. We can't go anywhere without having our feet on the ground; yet if we fall, we don't just lie there, sprawled in the dust. Our imperfections force us to acknowledge our misery, give us practice in humility, selflessness, patience, and watchfulness; yet, notwithstanding, God looks at the preparation of our heart and sees that it is perfect" (Marie Thibert, *Golden Counsels of SFS,* 13-14).

Prayer: Lord Jesus, thank You for Your call to remain ever-prepared. Help me to understand the importance of Your present day visitation, so that I may be always ready to welcome You into my life.

First Sunday of Advent, Year B

Is 63:16–17, 19, 64:2–7; 1 Cor 1:3–9; Mk 13:33–37

Preparation: Take a few minutes of silence, setting aside all your worries and anxieties, and become aware of the divine presence.

Listening to God's Word: "Be watchful! Be alert! You do not know when the time will come. It is like a man traveling abroad. He leaves home and places his servants in charge, each with his work, and orders the gatekeeper to be on the watch. Watch, therefore; you do not know when the lord of the house is coming, whether in the evening, or at midnight, or at cockcrow, or in the morning. May he not come suddenly and find you sleeping" (Mk 13:33–36).

Waiting for the day of the Lord

Our everyday experience shows that we are accustomed to do things according to our pre-planned schedules and appointments. If someone wants to meet us or if we plan to visit our friends and dear ones, we make prior appointments and work with our schedules. However, our God, Who loves us with unconditional love, does not follow a schedule or timetable to visit us. Hence, the Liturgy of the Word, at the beginning of the Advent season, tries to get us out of our humdrum and chronological perspective by emphasizing the need to be alert and watchful for the day of the Lord. When will that be? We don't know. It is an unknown time without a known plan or date, yet it is the Lord's *kairos,* "the appointed time." It is a time of hope-filled waiting. Jesus says, "Be watchful! Be alert! You do not know when the time will come" (Mk 13:33). The parable of the master in the Gospel narrative explains the serious implication of the Day of the Lord, which may come at anytime, anywhere, and in any moment (v. 35). Therefore, what is demanded is that, like the servants of the master, the disciples are to be alert and watchful by fulfilling their given responsibilities and earnestly waiting to encounter the Lord at all times. It shows that each moment of our present life is important, as it is a time of longing and waiting in hope-filled watchfulness.

This experience of waiting carries its own tension and excitement, as it involves the fulfillment of our expectations and goals, accomplishing our desires and aspirations. This experience of waiting in our Christian spirituality has deeper meaning, as it involves waiting in hope for the Lord's coming. Pope Francis says, "God always waits for us, even when we have left Him behind! He is never far from us, and if we return to Him, He is ready to embrace us." Hence, our hope-filled waiting to encounter Jesus in life implies an attitude of alertness and watchfulness, overcoming lethargy and disinterestedness. Since Jesus has entrusted His Gospel to the disciples that they may proclaim it until He comes, they are to live this present life by persevering in their faith, and being alert missionaries of the Gospel. This was the experience of Israel. Having admitted their sinfulness which separated them from the Lord (cf. Is 64:4b–5), they had turned to Him by gratefully recognizing His mighty deeds in the past, and longing for the powerful manifestation of His power once again in their present struggles (vv. 1–3, 7–8). Saint Paul, too, exhorted the Corinthian community to realize with gratitude that they had been enriched in every way and were not lacking in any spiritual gift (cf. 1 Cor 1:4–7). The members of the Corinthian community were reminded of their grave obligation to grow, as one community, in love and faithfulness, by proper use of their gifts; because, at the coming of the Lord, everyone will be called to account for how the gifts had nourished love and unity in the community. Therefore, Advent cannot simply be a following of some type of chronological calendar; rather it must remind us to be on the watch like a doorkeeper (Mk 13:35). Ask yourself: while waiting patiently, do I aspire to discern God's plan for me or ask God to fulfill my own interests? How meaningfully can I pray "Show me, O Lord, your face and grant me your salvation"?

Wisdom from St. Francis de Sales: "Reform your lives, and repent, says St. John; level all these mountains of pride, fill these valleys, these ravines of lethargy and of faint-heartedness. The valleys which this great saint wants us to fill are the valleys of fear, which lead us to discouragement at the sight of all the sins we commit. 'Fill the valleys means' fill your hearts with confidence and hope, because the sight of the great sins we have committed fills us with horror and dismay, with fear and terror which shatter the soul and lead it to discouragement" (SFS, *Conf. IX,* 443, from *Utilizing Our Faults,* 60).

Prayer: Jesus my Savior, You are my living hope. Guide me with Your grace to live by Your Gospel and proclaim it by a life of faith, persevering in my hope-filled waiting for Your coming.

First Sunday of Advent, Year C

Jer 33:14–16; 1 Thess 3:12–4:2; Lk 21:25–28, 34–36

Preparation: Take a few minutes of silence, setting aside all your worries and anxieties, and become aware of the divine presence.

Listening to God's Word: "But when these signs begin to happen, stand erect and raise your heads because our redemption is at hand...Beware that your hearts do not become drowsy from carousing and drunkenness and the anxieties of daily life, and that day catch you by surprise like a trap...Be vigilant at all times and pray that you have the strength to escape the tribulations..." (Lk 21:28, 34, 36).

Awareness of the Lord's nearness

There is a story narrated by Fr. Anthony de Mello (I have paraphrased it for the present reflection) that explains the focus of today's Liturgy of the Word, inviting us to be aware of Jesus' nearness in our life: Once, a priest announced in the church that Jesus Himself was coming to the parish the following Sunday. The people were so excited and turned up in large numbers to see Jesus face to face. When Jesus finally came, everyone expected Him to give a long sermon, but He just smiled when introduced. The parishioners offered Him hospitality for His stay overnight, but He gently refused, preferring to spend the night in the church. The people thought that was the fitting place for Him. Unfortunately, He slipped away early in the morning from the church, before the doors were opened. To their surprise, the whole church had been vandalized. Scratched everywhere were the two words "Be aware." No place was spared—the walls, the doors, the windows, the pillars, the altar, the pulpit, and even the Bible. People could see everywhere the words, "Be aware, Be aware, Be aware." What were they supposed to "be aware" of? It did not say. It was irritating and shocking for them. The first impulse of the people was to wipe out every trace of this defilement. However, they were restrained by a little girl who suggested, "Why don't we leave it as it is in memory of the visitation of Jesus to our church?" Now, whenever they came to church, those mysterious words began to sink into the hearts and minds of the people. So they began to be aware of the Scriptures, sacraments, religion, church laws and their faith in

God. Consequently, they were sanctified without becoming superstitious and self-righteous. They inscribed those miraculous words in big letters in their homes and began to be aware of their responsibilities and daily obligations. That made all the difference in their lives.

At the beginning of the season of Advent, we hear Jesus exhorting us, "Stand erect and raise your heads because your redemption is at hand" (Lk 21:28). These words are full of deep meaning, and serve as the rousing rhythm of the Advent season. Jesus cautions us to have proper attitudes and interior dispositions that will enable us to face the distressing events in the world with courage, standing erect in hope when the Lord comes (v. 36). So He teaches us to be aware, to be vigilant, and to pray. It emphasizes the need for an ever-preparedness filled with hope. Believers are to keep praying always, not allowing their hearts to be weighed down by carousing and drunkenness, or by the pleasures and distractions of daily life (v. 34). It is a practical admonition to be vigilant, that as disciples of Jesus we may not be over-confident or disinterested about the Lord's nearness. Jeremiah's prophecy is full of hope. Though the moral life of God's people was corrupt and characterized by shame and sham, still the prophet spoke to them about the promise of a new branch from David that would make the virtues of justice, truth, and integrity the center of people's relationships with God and with one another (cf. Jer 33:14–16). Saint Paul teaches us to grow in love for one another and to be blameless in our life of holiness (cf. 1 Thess 3:12–13), and thus to be aware of the Lord's nearness in the present moment. Ask yourself: like the people in the story, can I take to heart the Lord's command to "Be aware and be vigilant" in my life?

Wisdom from St. Francis de Sales: "In the course of the day, recall to mind the presence of God as often as you can. Become aware of what God is doing and of what you are doing: you will realize that His eyes are turned towards you and with unparalleled love fixed on you all the time. Philothea, our hearts must find and choose some place each day, either on Mount Calvary or in the words of our Lord, or in some other place near Him. There we must seek refuge at every opportunity" (SFS, *IDL, Part II*, Ch. 11, 127, 128).

Prayer: Lord Jesus, You are my strength in weakness. Grant me Your grace, so that my Advent preparation will be an experience of Your nearness, and that I might joyfully welcome You into my life.

Second Sunday of Advent, Year A

Is 11:1–10; Rom 15:4–9; Ps 72; Mt 3:1–12

Preparation: Take a few minutes of silence, setting aside all your worries and anxieties, and become aware of the divine presence.

Listening to God's Word: "When he saw many of the Pharisees and Sadducees coming to his baptism he said to them, 'You brood of vipers! Who warned you to flee from the coming wrath? Produce good fruit as evidence of your repentance. And do not presume to say to yourselves, "We have Abraham as our father"'" (Mt 3:7–9a).

Renewed life – the fruit of true repentance

There is a saying: "I changed my attitudes and so everything changed." This is the message of today's Liturgy of the Word, which focuses on the changing of one's attitudes and approaches toward life as a result of true repentance. Once, a tourist said to his guide, "You must be proud of your town and the people. I am so impressed and touched by the number of churches in your town, and amazed at the devotion of your people. Surely, this shows how much the people love the Lord." The guide replied cynically, "Very well, they may love the Lord, but sure indeed they hate each other as hell" (De Mello, *Song of the Bird*, 149). Through his preaching, Saint John challenged the various groups of people, inviting them to go through the process of renewal in life. By publicly calling the honorable religious leaders a "brood of vipers" (Mt 3:7), he directly challenged their claim to social honor and their biological claim to Abraham as their Father (v. 9). Through his preaching, he urged them to have a moral basis through sincere repentance and renewal in life. Therefore, the Baptist said, "Produce good fruit as evidence of your repentance" (v. 8). The people's acceptance of John's baptism through repentance was their radical turning away from disloyalty, to return to faithful obedience to God; this was a sign of their new life. Isaiah beautifully envisioned this perfect order of grace: "The wolf and lamb shall live together; the leopard and the child will play together, the calf and the lion will sleep together; the child will play with cobras. There shall be no harm or ruin on the Lord's holy mountain" (Is 11:6–9). There shall be no enmity and hatred, no vengeance and violence, no manipulation and destruction. There will be only peace and joy, unity and fraternal solidarity, blessings and prosperity, because of God's reign among us.

Jesus, as the long expected Messiah, inaugurated this new age by His incarnation. As believers, we are called to work together for the realization of this happy balance in our world, and to journey toward its final fulfillment. Today, we hear the slogan, "If you want peace, prepare for war, using any means." Such situations show that God's perfect order of grace and peace is manipulated and distorted in our personal life, in our families, and in our faith communities. There can be only wheat or chaff, acceptance or rejection. There can be no middle path. As a sign of our renewed life, we must love and welcome one another as Jesus has welcomed us into God's family (cf. Rom 15:4–9). Our acts of repentance must lead us to live a new life of goodness and kindness that is oriented toward the restoration of a perfect order of harmony and peace among us. We should practice reconciliation and forgiveness toward each other, and thus overcome the barriers that separate and divide us from God and from others. During this Advent season, let us ask ourselves: "The Messiah is around; when did I see him last?" Let us allow this question to resound in our hearts and minds, so that it will lead us to live a renewed life as the fruit of true repentance. Let's know that the ax is already at the root of the trees that do not produce good fruit (cf. Mt 3:10). Ask yourself: what is my response to Jesus' call to repentance? Am I ready to live a renewed life of repentance by living with a hope-filled attitude, and igniting the light of my faith, that it may burn brightly?

Wisdom from St. Francis de Sales: "Persevere in overcoming yourself in the little everyday frustrations that bother you; let your best efforts be directed there. God wishes nothing else of you at present, so don't waste time doing anything else. Don't sow your desires in someone else's garden; just cultivate your own as best you can; don't long to be other than what you are, but desire to be thoroughly what you are. Direct your thoughts to being very good at that and to bearing the crosses, little or great, that you will find there. We all love what is according to our taste; few people like what is according to their duty or to God's liking" (Marie Thibert, *Letters of Spiritual Direction,* 112).

Prayer: Lord Jesus, thank You for the voice of Saint John the Baptist, calling me to bear fruits of repentance. Help me to practice reconciliation, and become worthy to welcome You joyfully.

Second Sunday of Advent, Year B

Is 40:1–5, 9–11; 2 Pet 3:8–14; Mk 1:1–8

Preparation: Take a few minutes of silence, setting aside all your worries and anxieties, and become aware of the divine presence.

Listening to God's Word: "A voice of one crying out in the desert: 'Prepare the way of the Lord, make straight His paths.' John (the) Baptist appeared in the desert proclaiming a baptism of repentance for the forgiveness of sins. People of the whole Judean countryside and all the inhabitants of Jerusalem were going out to him and were being baptized by him in the Jordan river as they acknowledged their sins" (Mk 1:3–5).

Our identity: the Gospel

Every celebration in our family and each event in our society, whether religious or social, happens with adequate preparation and systematic arrangement. Such elaborate preparations show the importance of the event. As we prepare, during this Advent season, to celebrate the birth of Jesus, today's Liturgy of the Word urges us to understand the great significance of this divine event, and the need for adequate preparation so that God will find us worthy and blameless. In this way, we discover our true identity to be the Gospel of God's love in our world. Once, a friend wanted to meet another friend of his and when he arrived he noticed that the door was closed. So he called out, "Is anyone there, please?" There came a voice saying, "Hello, what do you want?" It was a child who responded while hiding. The man, presuming that it was the child of his friend, asked, "Is your daddy home?" "Yes," whispered the child. "Can I talk to him?" "No," the voice replied. "Is your mother there?" he asked. "Yes," came the answer. "Can I talk to her?" Again the voice whispered, "No." "All right. Is there anyone else beside you?" "Yes," whispered the child, "there is a police man." "A police man. Can I speak to him?" "No, he's busy," replied the child, still whispering. "Busy doing what?" he asked. "Talking to my daddy and mommy and the fireman," came the answer. "The fireman. Has there been a fire in the house or something?" asked the worried friend. "No," whispered the child. "Then what are the police and fireman doing here?" The voice whispered, "Don't shout. They are all searching for me."

During this Advent season, do we allow God to find us worthy of his love, or deliberately hide ourselves by denying our personal sins and neglecting our Christian commitment to be the Gospel of Jesus Christ? The call of Saint John the Baptist is an opportunity for us to discover our true identity and our need for God. As we heard from the Gospel narrative, Saint John was preaching a call to repentance for the forgiveness of sins, and proclaiming the imminent coming of the Messiah (cf. Mk 1:3). By calling the people into the desert, Saint John was calling them to discover and let go of their false hopes and securities, their selfish desires and ambitions. He encouraged them to discover God's promise of new life, to learn to hope and trust in God alone, so that God could find them faithful and trustworthy. Isaiah preached a message of hope to his depressed countrymen who, in their wounded experience of Babylonian exile circa 540 B.C., were driven into despair and discouragement. However, the prophet preached a message of comfort, urging them to discover that their own sins caused their present predicament of suffering. He invited them to know that a new period in their life was unfolding, that their punishment was over and their sins forgiven (cf. Is 40:1–2). He encouraged the people to discover the presence of the Lord even in the midst of oppression and pain. Christmas means experiencing God in our life. We are called to live by our identity as the Gospel of God's presence among us. Ask yourself: do I still hear the words of the prophet? Do I announce the Gospel of God's love, pointing out Jesus to the people around me, or do I turn them away from Him?

Wisdom from St. Francis de Sales: "Why should you trouble yourself with wanting or not wanting the events and mishaps of the world, since you don't know what you ought to wish for and God will always want for you what you would want yourself without your having to worry about it. Therefore, await peacefully the effects of the divine pleasure and let His will suffice, for it is always good. God told His beloved Saint Catherine of Siena, 'Think of me and I will think of you'" (Marie Thibert, *Golden Counsels of SFS,* 7-9).

Prayer: Loving God, thank You for revealing Your love and kindness. Grant me Your grace, to live by my identity as the Gospel of Jesus Christ, and to herald the gift of Your salvation for all.

Second Sunday of Advent, Year C

Bar 5:1–9; Phil 1:4–6, 8–11; Lk 3:1–6

Preparation: Take a few minutes of silence, setting aside all your worries and anxieties, and become aware of the divine presence.

Listening to God's Word: "He went throughout the whole region of the Jordan, proclaiming a baptism of repentance for the forgiveness of sins, as it is written in the book of the words of the prophet Isaiah, 'A voice of one crying out in the desert: prepare the way of the Lord, make straight his paths. Every valley shall be filled and every mountain and hill shall be made low. The winding roads shall be made straight, and rough ways made smooth, and all flesh shall see the salvation of God'" (Lk 3:3-6).

Preparing the way of the Lord

When we are faced with problems and issues either in our family life or personal life, we usually prefer to have some quiet moments, in order to be alone for prayer and introspection. In such grace-filled moments, we receive new insights, and a new orientation. That is why the ancient philosophers taught that "The unexamined life is not worth living." Saint John the Baptist, as the forerunner of the Messiah, insists on the need for self-reflection. Therefore he cried out, "[P]repare the way of the Lord, make straight his paths. Every valley shall be filled and every mountain and hill shall be made low. The winding roads shall be made straight, and the rough ways made smooth, and all flesh will see the salvation of God" (Lk 3:5ff). This Isaiahan prophecy was actually concerned with the return of Israel from Babylonian exile; it offered them the message of hope and consolation. The mountains and hills, the valleys and rough roads, are the realities that cause disorder and chaos in our personal life and in our family. They are symbols of all that creates a situation of schizophrenia in our society. At the messianic breakthrough caused by the coming of the Messiah, there will be a complete change in the lives of people and in society. The images of flattening the high mountains, filling out the valleys and smoothing the rough roads, signify the creation of this new order.

We might be familiar with the famous painting by Holman Hunt, entitled "The Light of the World." It portrays Jesus, crowned with thorns and standing before a house with a lantern in his hand, knocking at the closed door. There is no handle on the door. Someone asked the artist the reason for not painting a handle on the door. He replied that the handle is on the inside of the door; that we must take the initiative ourselves to open the door for Jesus, the Light. It is very true. Jesus the Messiah can only knock at the door and offer the opportunity. We must come forward to open the door for the grace which Jesus offers. There is a real possibility for true repentance and renewal in life. There is a saying: "Transformed humanity is a reconciled humanity, and reformed personality is a renewed and integrated personality." This is the result of the grace-filled act of introspection and renewal in life. By critical self-reflection on our own decisions and actions, we will gain new perspectives that will motivate us to determine what is best for us and for the community. We will be encouraged to grow deeper in our love for God and one another (cf. Phil 1:10–11). It will help us to produce in abundance the fruits of righteousness, and to see the salvation of God (cf. Lk 3:6). The prophet Baruch spoke to the people of Israel about their own restoration, and encouraged them to keep their hope alive as preparation for that great messianic day that was yet to come (cf. Bar 5:5–6). Jesus, as the light on our journey, guides us in our daily struggles and troubles, and constantly calls us to renewal. Ask yourself: do I listen to the voice of Jesus and open the door for Him? Am I aware of the rough roads and crooked ways in life, and do I recognize my need for renewal?

Wisdom from St. Francis de Sales: "John the Baptist preached, 'Do penance and make straight the way of the Lord, fill up the valleys, lower the mountains and hills. They, as well as the ditches and valleys, trouble travelers. Make straight the paths, those that twist and turn fatigue the pilgrim greatly. Our life too contains many hills, valleys and tortuous ways which can be put right only by penitence. Penitence fills up the valleys, lays low the mountains, makes straight and smooths the ways; lower those mountains of pride, fill up those valleys, those ditches of lukewarmness and tepidity'" (Visitation, *The Sermons of SFS for Advent and Christmas,* 45).

Prayer: Lord Jesus, thank You for helping me to understand my need for self-examination. Guide me to discover the valleys, the rough ways, and the ditches in my life, that I might be renewed.

Third Sunday of Advent, Year A

Is 35:1–6, 10; James 5:7–10; Mt 11:2–11

Preparation: Take a few minutes of silence, setting aside all your worries and anxieties, and become aware of the divine presence.

Listening to God's Word: "Go and tell John what you hear and see: the blind regain their sight, the lame walk, lepers are cleansed, the deaf hear, the dead are raised, the poor have the good news proclaimed to them. And blessed is the one who takes no offense at me" (Mt 11:4–6).

Proclaiming a message of hope

The spiritual Master kept saying to everyone, "God loves the people in their suffering as much as in their success. If God loves us in the worst, then we are the living Gospel of hope." This sums up the thrust of today's Liturgy of the Word, which comes as good news of hope to those who are afflicted and in despair. When Israel was defeated and taken into exile in Babylon, the people asked the questions, "Is our God powerful or weak? If He is a powerful God, how can He be silent, allowing such a terrible tragedy to happen to His chosen people?" They wondered whether God would start all over again to bring them liberation. To the discouraged and fearful people in exile, the prophet proclaimed the message of hope: that Yahweh had not forgotten them. In fact, He would lead them back home. This journey of coming back from exile would be their second exodus into the homeland of success and prosperity, joy and happiness. Here four categories of people are singled out, namely, the deaf, the blind, the lame, and the dumb. These categories underline the pitiable condition of God's people (cf. Is 43:8). However, the disenfranchised people of God have their claim on Him who will surely defend and protect them. The basic motive for such a marvelous display of God's concern is His unconditional love (cf. Is 43:4). Therefore, the prophet proclaimed the words of hope: "Be strong, fear not. Here is your God...he comes to save you" (Is 35:4). This saving act of God is demonstrated very concretely by Jesus. So He answered the disciples who carried the question from John the Baptist (who was in prison), "Go and tell John what you hear and see: the blind regain their sight, the lame walk, lepers are cleansed, the deaf hear, the dead are raised, and the poor have the good news proclaimed to them" (cf. Mt 11:3–5). By doing the activities of the Messiah, Jesus proved His identity: that He is the Messiah, "the one who is to come" (Mt 11:3), inaugurating the time of salvation for all.

As Messiah, He gives life to those who are lifeless, and offers hope to those who are groping in the darkness of despair. We witness in our world today that in spite of tremendous growth and enormous wealth, millions of our brothers and sisters suffer poverty, corruption, ill-treatment, and various diseases. People become innocent victims of violence, injustice, oppression, manipulation, and subjugation. In such situations of pain and suffering, God's word comes to us as a word of hope: "Be strong; do not be afraid. The Lord comes to save you." Jesus is the source of our joy and hope. Pope Benedict XVI says, "With the angel's greeting to Mary—'kaire' which means 'be joyful'—the New Testament begins. We could say that the first word of the New Testament is 'be joyful,' 'be happy,' in other words, 'joy.' This is the true meaning of Christmas: God is near us, so near that He became a child. Our world today, where God is absent, is dominated by fear and uncertainty. Nonetheless, the words 'be joyful because God is with us,' truly open a new time." In fact, Advent stirs up our hope, motivating us to incarnate hope in our lives by acts of kindness. We cannot be mere recipients of the good news of hope. We also must become messengers of hope in our world. Ask yourself: in what ways do I experience that God is truly present in my life? Do I create a situation of hopelessness and vulnerability for people, or do I help them to live in hope?

Wisdom from St. Francis de Sales: "You should never get discouraged. All that you are expected to do is to have a courage that is gentle and patient and take your time and all the care needed to heal and comfort your heart in the wake of the assaults it has endured. Have courage. Let us do our best, all we possibly can, and God will be happy with us. It is one thing sometimes to be beaten and quite another thing to be vanquished" (SFS, *Conf. XVI,* 63; *VI,* 378, from *The Art of Utilizing Our Faults,* 47, 49).

Prayer: Lord Jesus, You are my joy and hope. Guide me with Your grace to be a person of optimism, that I may keep my faith alive and bring others the message of hope to find new life.

Third Sunday of Advent, Year B

Is 61:1–2, 10–11; 1 Thess 5:16–24; Jn 1:6–8, 19–28

Preparation: Take a few minutes of silence, setting aside all your worries and anxieties, and become aware of the divine presence.

Listening to God's Word: "A man named John was sent from God. He came for testimony, to testify to the light, so that all might believe through him. He was not the light, but came to testify to the light…John answered them, 'I baptize with water; but there is one among you whom you do not recognize, the one who is coming after me, whose sandal strap I am not worthy to untie'" (Jn 1:6–8, 26–27).

Following the light

Light occupies a very important place in human life. Just imagine what we would do without light. The whole world would be plunged into utter darkness. However, what brightens things up, making human life meaningful and worth living, is the light of our conscience, and God's grace within us, which prompts us to live by our faith-values and convictions. Once, the spiritual Master said to the disciples, "Light is reflected on the wall. But why, to venerate the wall? Just be attentive to the Light. You will be enlightened and know the truth." Jesus Christ is our light. As believers, we are called to persevere in our life journey by walking in His light. Saint John the Baptist came as a witness and exhorted the people to follow the light of Jesus. As we are earnestly preparing to experience Jesus this Advent, we must listen to Saint John's proclamation: "There is one among you whom you do not recognize, the one who is coming after me" (Jn 1:26–27). The focus of this announcement is that Jesus is here in our midst, and we are called to recognize and accept Him as the light of our life. This is what we hear from Isaiah who proclaimed the Messiah's program of liberation. His audience was the depressed and dejected post-exilic community; for it was to them that he announced the year of the Lord. It was a grace-filled time, when God repaired the injuries and healed the wounds suffered by His people.

However, Jesus, Who came as the True Light, is not a passive onlooker. As the expected Messiah, "He is sent to bring good news to the oppressed, to bind up the brokenhearted, to proclaim liberty to the captives, release to the prisoners and to comfort all those who mourn" (Is 61:1–2). It is a message of encouragement that sustains every believer's hope in God's promise of new life. Into this background, Jesus came, to offer us the light of grace that we may seek God's gift of salvation. It is this Jesus Who comes as the Light into our life, daily enlightening us to walk in the way of truth. As Saint Paul instructs us, the appropriate attitude must be "to rejoice always, praying unceasingly and giving thanks for everything" (1 Thess 5:26–28). It implies an optimistic approach to life, discerning God's plans and facing life experiences with positive attitudes. It will be the joyful moment of experiencing Jesus in our lives' events. Following John's faith-witness, we are called to live by the light of Jesus, and to give witness to the Lord in our world. God's presence is always a dynamic, participating presence and is never a static, controlling presence. Hence, we must make efforts in our personal life to dispel the darkness of our selfishness, our pride, our attitudes of hatred and attachment to materialism, by following the light of the Messiah. In our families and faith-communities, everyone must strive to overcome the attitudes of misunderstanding, unfaithfulness, lethargy, and disinterestedness; we must care for each other in order to live by the light of Jesus. Ask yourself: do I reject Jesus in my life, or walk with Him by living in His light? Do I recognize God's involvement in my life, rejoicing always, praying without ceasing, and thanking God for His many blessings?

Wisdom from St. Francis de Sales: "Observe how kind Divine Providence is to us! God encourages us to have confidence in Him. A son will never perish while he is in the arms of his Almighty Father. If God does not always give us what we ask, He only does this to keep us near Him. He wants us to ask Him for help, storming heaven with a loving violence. He is kind and merciful. As soon as we submit ourselves to His will, He immediately grants our wishes" (SFS, *Letters, 1513: O. XVIII,* from *Every Day with SFS,* 90).

Prayer: God of Mercy, thank You for sending Jesus as the light of our world. Grant me the grace to walk in His light, and to overcome the hurdles in my faith-journey with a positive attitude.

Third Sunday of Advent, Year C

Zeph 3:14–18a; Phil 4:4–7; Lk 3:10–18

Preparation: Take a few minutes of silence, setting aside all your worries and anxieties and become aware of the divine presence.

Listening to God's Word: "And the crowds asked [John the Baptist], 'What then should we do?' He said to them in reply, 'Whoever has two cloaks should share with the person who has none. And whoever has food should do likewise.' Even the tax collectors came to be baptized and they said to him, 'Teacher, what should we do?' He answered them, 'Stop collecting more than what is prescribed.' Soldiers also asked him, 'And what is it that we should do?' He told them, 'Do not practice extortion, do not falsely accuse anyone, and be satisfied with your wages'" (Lk 3:10–14).

What should we do?

Saint John the Baptist, appearing as a prophet after four hundred years of Israel's prophetic history, preached a message of repentance which provoked the people to self-examination, leading them to renewal in life. Once, four young men who were non-believers approached a priest and asked, "What should we do to be saved? Somebody told us to study the Bible, learn the catechism of the Church, know about the faith and be baptized. Can you help us?" The priest said, "Sure, I can teach you about the Bible and help you to learn about the faith. It's not a problem. You come back after a month. But you should know one thing: that when you return after a month, one of you will be dead." The four young men came back as the priest directed but nothing had happened to them. Therefore, they asked the priest, "You said that one of us would be dead after a month but nothing happened to us." Then the priest asked them, "What did you do during this one month?" They replied, "Since you said that one of us would be dead within a month, we were frightened. So we did our best to behave well, helping others, and living a good life by doing righteous deeds as often as we could." The priest said, "If you could do such righteous deeds for the rest of your life, you would be saved. This is true catechism." This conveys the central point of today's Gospel, which teaches the practical dimension of true repentance. The suddenness of John's appearance in the wilderness—living with remarkable austerity—and his mighty voice, jolted the people from their listlessness. The fact that the same question was raised by three different groups of people (cf. Lk 3:10, 12, 14) shows that his message provoked them to reflect on their own lives. Therefore, they asked him, "What should we do?" This is a powerful question of self-realization.

The answer from Saint John concerns the social character of repentance. He exhorted his listeners to share their clothes and food with those who had none, to stop collecting more than what was prescribed, to avoid extortion, to not falsely accuse anyone, and to be satisfied with their wages (cf. Lk 3:10–14). Saint Paul exhorts us, "Your kindness should be known to all" (Phil 4:5). This describes the program of mercy and love toward others which is a reflection of true repentance. Saint Paul further says, "Whatever is honorable, whatever is just, whatever is lovely, whatever is gracious, if there is anything excellent and worthy of praise, think about these things" (cf. Phil 4:8). Such an attitude of other-centeredness would motivate us to realize God's presence among us. We can learn to "rejoice and sing joyfully" because "God our Savior is in our midst" (Zeph 3: 14–16). As we are preparing with excitement and expectancy to celebrate the birth of our Savior, we must ask the question: What should I do to renew any broken relationships and to restore happiness in my family? What should I do to deepen my love for the Lord and grow in righteousness? Let the question "What, then, shall I do?" lead us to practical commitments for a renewed life, that we may experience Jesus and become better persons.

Wisdom from St. Francis de Sales: "Lower the mountains and hills. What are these mountains but presumption and pride, which are very great obstacles to our Lord's coming? He humbles and lowers the haughty (Matt 23:12; Lk 1:52; 18:14) and penetrates the depths of the heart to discover the pride that lies hidden there. It is useless to say to Him, 'I am a bishop, a priest, a religious.' Well and good; but if you are a bishop, how do you conduct yourself in this ministry? What is your life like; are your morals congruent with your vocation?" (Visitation, *The Sermons of SFS for Advent and Christmas,* 46).

Prayer: Lord God, thank You for Your promise of new life. Guide me to follow the exhortation of Saint John the Baptist to speak and do in life whatever is life-giving, honorable, and lovable.

Fourth Sunday of Advent, Year A

Is 7:10–14; Rom 1:1–7; Mt 1:18–24

Preparation: Take a few minutes of silence, setting aside all your worries and anxieties, and become aware of the divine presence.

Listening to God's Word: "Joseph her husband, since he was a righteous man, yet unwilling to expose her to shame, decided to divorce her quietly…When Joseph awoke, he did as the angel of the Lord had commanded him and took his wife into his home" (Mt 1:19, 24).

Human response important for divine response

The Scriptures teach us that God has acted in salvation history according to the faith-response of the people. Abraham (cf. Gen 12:1–4), Moses (cf. Ex 3:10–12, 4:18–20), the prophets (cf. 1 Sam 3:3–10; Is 6:8–9; Jer 1:4–10), Saint Paul (cf. Rom 1:1), and others, responded to God's call in total surrender for the fulfillment of God's plan for our salvation. Saint Joseph and the Virgin Mary responded to God's call without resistance or reservations, which resulted in the Incarnation of Jesus as Emmanuel (cf. Mt 1:25). Thus, they each made a difference. Such human responses involve a radical leap of faith in total surrender to God. The Gospel narrative today focuses on the faith-response of Saint Joseph. He is presented as a righteous man (cf. Mt 1:19) who observed, in loyalty, the Law and his Jewish religious traditions. When God's divine plan for the salvation of humanity was revealed to him, Joseph had in front of him only two options: either to accept God's plan for the birth of the Messiah by accepting Mary, who was conceived by the power of the Holy Spirit, or to expose her to disgrace. For Joseph, this was a crucial moment of decision-making. He had to go through the agony of wrestling with such a difficult decision in deciding for, or against, God's plan. Pope Benedict XVI says, "Joseph's silence in the Gospel does not demonstrate an empty interior, but rather the fullness of faith that he carries in his heart. Let's allow ourselves to be 'infected' by the silence of St. Joseph! Silence is so lacking in this world which is often too noisy, which is not favorable to recollection and listening to the voice of God. In this time of preparation for Christmas, let us cultivate interior recollection so as to receive and keep Jesus in our lives."

Joseph, being a righteous man, did not want to put others to shame; so he tried to solve this problem by quietly divorcing Mary (cf. v. 19b). His deep faith in God seemed to have brought him more troubles than blessings. Yet, Joseph's faith-struggle informs us that trouble may surround us when God enters into our life. From our experiences we also know that our sincere commitment to God and neighbor may bring with it, at times, stings and arrows of even outrageous and unexpected troubles and hardships. We might struggle like Joseph in all such moments. However, God guided Joseph in his struggles, assuring him, "Do not be afraid to take Mary your wife into your home. For it is through the Holy Spirit that this child has been conceived in her" (Mt 1:20). Surely, God's blessings may be hidden in the darkness of our troubles and trials. Moreover, when Joseph understood God's plan for human salvation, he responded freely and played a responsible role. By accepting Mary and her divinely-conceived Child, Joseph totally surrendered to God's will. Similarly, God can come to us most powerfully in the midst of our own troubles, promising us divine guidance; provided that we respond to God's will like Saint Joseph, in uncompromising faith and trust. Through his free response, Joseph made possible the emergence of God's nearness in Jesus as Emmanuel. This shows that our God is a God of great surprises. When we follow Him in total surrender and commit ourselves to fulfilling His divine plan, God will surprise us in amazing ways, through unexpected displays of His many blessings. Ask yourself: how do I accept and respond to God's plan for me? Can I follow Jesus in complete trust, even in the darkest moments of my life?

Wisdom from St. Francis de Sales: "It is very true that in order to surrender ourselves unreservedly to divine providence, we ourselves have to be very trusting. But it is also true that when we let go of everything, our Lord takes care of all and manages all. If we hold back anything—this shows a lack of trust in Him—He lets us keep it. It is as if He said, 'You think yourself wise enough to handle this matter without me; I allow you to do so; you will see how you come out in the end'" (Marie Thibert, *Golden Counsels of SFS,* 20).

Prayer: Lord God, You are gracious and merciful. Guide me to accept Your divine plan in complete trust as Saint Joseph did, and to experience Your blessings in moments of struggle.

Fourth Sunday of Advent, Year B

2 Sam 7:1–5, 8–12, 14, 16; Rom 16:25–27; Lk 1:26–38

Preparation: Take a few minutes of silence, setting aside all your worries and anxieties, and become aware of the divine presence.

Listening to God's Word: "But Mary said to the angel, 'How can this be, since I have no relations with a man?' And the angel said to her in reply, 'The Holy Spirit will come upon you, and the power of the Most High will overshadow you. Therefore the child to be born will be called holy, the Son of God.' Mary said, 'Behold, I am the handmaid of the Lord. May it be done to me according to your word'" (Lk 1:34–35, 38).

Holy people…holy temple

Today's temples are a sacred place of worship, and the symbol of God's living presence in every religion that fosters people's religious customs and traditions. In ancient Israel, too, the temple figured prominently as a symbol defining their self-understanding to be a chosen people. While we build massive structures for God as holy temples (churches), God in fact desires to form the people themselves to become holy and righteous. Today's Liturgy of the Word captures the meaning of this theme by focusing on the role of the Virgin Mary as the temple of God. It was the faith-conviction of Israel that God had chosen them out of all the peoples on earth "to be a special people, God's treasured possession" (Deut 7:6–8). Their election as a chosen people implied that they were to be holy to the Lord, so that they could experience His life-giving presence among them. This was their experience in the desert, where the Ark of the Covenant was a symbol of God's true presence in their midst. It was in this context that David wanted to build a temple (a house) for God. But the Lord was not so interested in the magnificent material structure of a temple; rather He wanted to build a house of people through David's descendants (cf. 2 Sam 7:11–12). They were to be God's special possession, as His agents of salvation in human history. The early Church also claimed its identity as a "chosen people." All who believe in Jesus become God's chosen people, full of grace. Therefore, Saint Peter the Apostle beautifully proclaims, "But you are 'a chosen race, a royal priesthood, a holy nation, a people of his own, so that you may announce the praises' of him who has called you out of darkness into his wonderful light" (1 Pet 2:9).

Every believer in Jesus, through his or her baptism, is called to be God's holy temple. "Chosen by God" means "favored one," cared for and protected by God in a special way. Moreover, the Virgin Mary, full of grace, represents such a chosen people of God. Receiving the Messiah into her womb, she became God's temple and the new Ark of the Covenant. Therefore, as the angel said, the Holy Spirit overshadowed her and the glory of God rested on her (cf. Lk 1:35; 1 Kg 8:10–11; Ex 33:9–11). Vatican II has succinctly summarized Mary's response as follows: "At the message of the angel the Virgin Mary received the Word of God in her heart and in her body, and gave life to the world" (Constitution on the Church, 53). When Mary responded, "Behold, I am the handmaid of the Lord. May it be done to me according to your word" (Lk 1:38), she in fact wholeheartedly accepted her call to be the mother of the Savior, with all its implications. "Handmaid of the Lord" implies "belonging to God alone." It is expressed in terms of being available to, and accepting, God's will. Mary did just that as God's holy temple. Moreover, Mary's response reminds us that our election as a people of God is a call to BECOME God's holy temple. We are to live in faithfulness to God, Who will strengthen and guide us to proclaim Jesus as the Savior of the world (cf. Rom 16:25–26). God's presence within us, and around us, is real because our God, revealed in Jesus, is real. Mary experienced God's living presence in her life and she was full of grace because she let God work in her life. Ask yourself: am I aware of my election as a member of God's holy people, and do I allow God to work through me? Do I live according to my vocation to be God's living temple here on earth?

Wisdom from St. Francis de Sales: "See, then, Theotimus, how much God wants us to love Him. He is not satisfied with publicly announcing His intense desire to be loved, so that each one can share in His loving invitation. He even goes from door to door knocking and knocking. He assures that if anyone opens, He will come to him and eat with him [Rev 3:20], that is, He will show him all sorts of kindness" (SFS, *Treatise on the Love of God,* Vol. 1, Book II, Ch. 8, 109).

Prayer: Loving and merciful God, thank You for presenting Mary as Your holy temple. Help me to understand my call to be Your holy temple here on earth, diffusing Your goodness and love.

Fourth Sunday of Advent, Year C

Micah 5:1–4a; Heb 10:5–10; Lk 1:39–45

Preparation: Take a few minutes of silence, setting aside all your worries and anxieties, and become aware of the divine presence.

Listening to God's Word: "When Elizabeth heard Mary's greetings, the infant leaped in her womb, and Elizabeth, filled with the holy Spirit, cried out in a loud voice and said, 'Most blessed are you among women, and blessed is the fruit of your womb…Blessed are you who believed that what was spoken to you by the Lord would be fulfilled'" (Lk 1:41–42, 45).

The Visitation – an experience of shared faith

The experience of meeting people whom we love is always a special moment of grace and happiness. In that joyful encounter, we are encouraged, cheered up, and become persons with renewed spirits. That is the reason why it is said that the people who love people are the luckiest and the happiest people in the world. Saint Patrick says, "Christ with me, Christ before me, Christ behind me, Christ within me, Christ below me, Christ above me, Christ at my right, Christ at my left, Christ in lying down, Christ in sitting, Christ in rising up, Christ in the heart of every man who thinks of me, Christ in the mouth of every man who speaks to me, Christ in every eye that sees me, Christ in every ear that hears me." This is what the Virgin Mary and Elizabeth experienced at their visitation. The visitation story is an inspiration for all of us in our faith-encounter with God and with other people. The Scriptures say that Mary and Elizabeth were righteous and blameless before God and people (cf. Lk 1:5–6, 27–28). As they were women of deep faith, God chose them to play important roles for the fulfillment of His plan in salvation history. Hence, the meeting of these two mothers was in fact the meeting of two worlds, namely, the world of messianic promise (prophecy) and the world of messianic fulfillment. Saint John the Baptist announced the coming of the Messiah, and Jesus, as the Messiah Himself, inaugurated the new age of salvation. Furthermore, the visitation of Mary with Elizabeth was not a casual meeting. Both of them had good news of great joy for each other, as they encountered God in their lives.

Mary went in haste to visit Elizabeth (v. 39) and share the good news of the Annunciation. Elizabeth, too, had good news for Mary. Moved by the Holy Spirit, she affirmed the identity of Mary as "the mother of my Lord" (v. 43) and her role as the blessed one "who believed that what was spoken…by the Lord would be fulfilled" (v. 45). Thus, their meeting was a faith-sharing experience of God's intervention in their lives. They prayed, rejoiced, and celebrated together the marvelous work of God which they experienced. Moreover, the significance of this visitation is the personal presence of these two mothers. Realizing that Elizabeth needed help, as she conceived in her old age, Mary undertook a challenging journey from Galilee to the hill country of Judea (vv. 39–40). It was indeed a dangerous undertaking, yet Mary wanted to be with her cousin, to share her joy and help her in difficult times. Therefore, Mary remained with Elizabeth for three months and helped her until Elizabeth gave birth (v. 56). Elizabeth, too, brought inspiration to the life of Mary by affirming and blessing her as the one who believed in the Lord's promise. Their personal presence was the greatest gift out of all that they shared with each other, especially in their difficult moments. As believers, they became messengers of the good news of joy to the world. Our daily visiting of friends and those who are suffering should be a grace-filled time of faith-sharing. Ask yourself: am I ready to give the gift of my personal presence to my parents, dear ones, and friends, in their most challenging times? Like Mary and Elizabeth, do I gratefully acknowledge God's involvement in my life, and inspire others with my own faith-experience?

Wisdom from St. Francis de Sales: "The virtue of devotion is nothing other than a general inclination and readiness of the soul to do what it knows to be agreeable to God. It is the joyful expansion of the heart spoken of in the Psalms: 'I have run in the way of your commandments since you have set me free.' Ordinary people walk along the path of God; but devout people run, and if they are very devout, they fly" (SFS, *Thy Will Be Done,* 6-7).

Prayer: Gracious God, thank You for inspiring me through the faith-sharing of the Virgin Mary and Saint Elizabeth. Guide me to share my faith, and to offer people encouragement and motivation by my visitation.

The Feast of the Immaculate Conception

Gen 3:9–15, 20; Eph 1:3–6, 11–12; Lk 1:26–38

Preparation: Take a few minutes of silence, setting aside all your worries and anxieties, and become aware of the divine presence.

Listening to God's Word: "Then the angel said to her, 'Do not be afraid, Mary, for you have found favor with God. Behold, you will conceive in your womb and bear a son, and you shall name him Jesus. He will be great and will be called Son of the Most High…' Mary said, 'Behold, I am the handmaid of the Lord. May it be done to me according to your word'" (Lk 1:30–32, 38).

Unconditional trust

John was his name. He was born into the noble family of Feretti in a small village in Italy. As a young boy, he was intelligent and very handsome, but he had epilepsy. He suffered greatly from this disease. So he fervently prayed to the Blessed Mother for a cure, and he was miraculously healed of his disease. In gratitude, he took the name of Mary as his middle name, and had great devotion to her. This boy was none other than Pope Pius IX, who proclaimed on December 8, 1854, that the "Immaculate Conception of the Blessed Virgin Mary" is a Dogma of the Catholic Faith. This Dogma teaches that "the blessed virgin Mary was from the first moment of her conception, by a singular grace and privilege of almighty God and by the merits of Jesus Christ, preserved immune from all stain of original sin" (*Catechism of the Catholic Church*, 491). In the first days of creation, Adam and Eve disobeyed God's commandment, aspiring to be equal with God. Their action ruptured humanity's relationship with God and introduced evil into the world. To reverse this distortion of creation, God began to unfold His plan of salvation, a plan that would offer humanity the gift of eternal life. To accomplish this purpose, God created some people to be outstanding in holiness, that they might play an important role as instruments in His hands. Mary was one of them. If Jesus Christ, the Savior of the world, was to redeem humanity from sin, then He could be born only from a woman who was perfectly free from every influence of sin. Therefore, God made Mary sinless from the beginning. There is a saying: "When people of pure heart are around, even the market place is as sacred as the sanctuary." This is very much true of Mary, our Blessed Mother. God does not want us only to be a beautiful vessel, but also to be persons of pure hearts. Mary was both a beautiful vessel and a woman of pure heart. Moreover we can learn from Mary a lesson about the virtue of unconditional trust in God, with purity of heart and mind.

The Psalmist says that the man with clean hands and a pure heart will receive blessings from the Lord (cf. Ps 24:3–6). Mary was such a person, pure of heart; she was a holy dwelling place for the Savior of the World to dwell in. She was full of grace (cf. Lk 1:28). That is why she wholeheartedly trusted all that was revealed to her by God, and believed in God's promise until the end. So she responded to God, saying, "Let it be done to me according to your word" (cf. Lk 1:38). Saint Paul teaches that we are chosen to be holy and blameless before him (Eph 1:3–4). The splendor of holiness with which Mary was enriched from the moment of her conception is entirely unique in nature. God the Father chose Mary and blessed her more than any other created person, through Christ Jesus, with a special grace before the foundation of the world, to be holy and blameless before Him. Thus, Mary is presented as the prime model for all believers in their call to holiness. We are urged today to follow the example of Mary in continuing our faith-journey and in our battle to overcome every influence of sin. Like her, we are called to submit in faith and trust to God's divine plans, which will bring many surprising blessings. Ask yourself: am I ready to accept God's plan with uncompromising trust? Can I respond to God's call in trust as Mary did, saying "Let it be done to me according to your will"?

Wisdom from St. Francis de Sales: "Our Lady, being reassured by the angel and having learned what God willed to do with her and in her, made this supreme act of humility, saying: I am the servant of the Lord. Let it be done to me as you say. She saw herself raised to the highest dignity that ever was or will be. This dignity is incomparable; and yet the sacred Virgin is not puffed up, but declares that she will always remain the servant of the Divine Majesty. Our Lady humbled herself and acknowledged herself unworthy of being raised to the high dignity of Mother of God; therefore she was made to be His Mother" (Lewis S. Fiorelli (ed.), *The Sermons of SFS on Our Lady*, 146-147).

Prayer: Gracious God, You created Mary sinless from the beginning to be the Mother of Jesus. Guide me with Your grace to be faithful in following Your divine will in total surrender.

Christmas - Mass During the Day

Is 52:7–10; Heb 1:1–6; Jn 1:1–18 or 1–5, 9–14

Preparation: Take a few minutes of silence, setting aside all your worries and anxieties, and become aware of the divine presence.

Listening to God's Word: "He came to what was his own, but his own people did not accept him. But to those who did accept him he gave power to become children of God, to those who believe in his name, who were born not by natural generation nor by human choice nor by a man's decision but of God. And the Word became flesh and made his dwelling among us, and we saw his glory, the glory as of the Father's only Son, full of grace and truth" (Jn 1:11–14).

He came to give us life

There is nothing so precious and valuable as human life, and there is nothing so manipulated and abused as human life. Today's feast of the birth of Jesus impels us to respect, honor, and celebrate the value of human life as God's precious gift. Once, there was a report in the newspaper about a young man named John who was very courageous and talented. He loved ice fishing. One day it happened that while fishing, the ice on the lake was broken, and John had slipped into the cold water. Screaming from the freezing water, he was struggling to survive. Fortunately, someone who was passing by heard the screams for help. This man rushed across the ice with a rope on his shoulder. In a few minutes, he got John out of the water and took him to the nearest hospital. Leaving the half-frozen and frightened John in the emergency room, the stranger shook hands with him and said, "Someday, you may find someone in need and you can help that person, too," and he left. Only then did John realize that he did not even know his rescuer's name. However, he acknowledged with gratitude the kindness and courage of that man who had saved his life. Furthermore, he thanked God for His miraculous intervention by saving him through a stranger, and he determined to reach out and bring life to those in need. Our Christmas celebration today brings us the same message. Jesus, Who is the Eternal Word, came to give us life; not like a stranger, but by becoming one of us. In the Gospel, Saint John explains that Jesus is the source of all life, and that everything came into existence through Him. "What came to be through him was life, and this life was the light of the human race" (John 1:3–4).

Jesus, the Divine Word, is the One Who communicates the life of the Father to us, and the manner of communicating the divine life is human. "The Word became flesh and made his dwelling among us" (v. 14). "To dwell" means that God literally pitched His tent among His people. It expresses the truth that the Eternal Word, Who is beyond time, has come within time in the person of Jesus, to live among us. It reminds us of God's dwelling among His people Israel in the tent (cf. Ex 40:34) where they experienced His living presence and saving power. Furthermore, Jesus our Savior, Who gave us life, did not go away like the stranger in the story above, leaving us alone; instead, He continues to live among us, and in spite of our imperfections and weaknesses, our sins and selfishness, our hopelessness and messiness, He continues to sanctify us. "The spirituality of the Nativity is used to describe the admirable exchange between the divine and the human. The first act of that exchange comes in Christ's own humanity. The Word assumed our humanity and, in exchange, human nature was raised to divine dignity. The second act of the exchange consists in our real and intimate involvement in the divine nature of the Word" (Pope Benedict XVI). The prophecy of Isaiah that Yahweh would comfort His people (cf. Is 40:1) has been fulfilled at the birth of Jesus, for all the ends of the earth have seen the salvation of our God. The Infant Jesus in the stable is God-in-the-flesh, God-one-of-us, our Emmanuel. Whatever Jesus said and did, there was life. Ask yourself: do I appreciate the gift of life and honor it? How do I help others to find meaning in life?

Wisdom from St. Francis de Sales: "A loving heart should strive more fervently to produce works of high value and quality in order to increase powerfully its charity. But even if it sometimes produces works of lesser value it will not lose its reward. God will be pleased with them. He will love the person a little more because of them. God never shows additional love to a soul already having charity without giving further charity to it. Our love for God is the appropriate and particular effect of His love for us" (SFS, *Treatise on the Love of God*, Vol. 1, Book III, Ch. 2, 166).

Prayer: Jesus my Savior, by Your Incarnation, You have united heaven and earth. Help me to become a channel of Your blessings, and to transmit life to whomever I encounter in life.

The Feast of the Holy Family

Sir 3:2–6, 12–14; Col 3:12–17; Mt 2:13-15, 19–23 (A),
Lk 2:22–40 (B), Lk 2:41–52 (C)

Preparation: Take a few minutes of silence, setting aside all your worries and anxieties, and become aware of the divine presence.

Listening to God's Word: "When they had fulfilled all the prescriptions of the law of the Lord, they returned to Galilee, to their own town of Nazareth. The child grew and became strong, filled with wisdom; and the favor of God was upon him" (Lk 2:39–40)

The family – God's temple on earth

Our common experience shows that a child experiences God's love first in the family, even before the child learns about a loving God. Therefore the saying is true that "The family that prays together stays together," and the family that fights together strays together. Once, an elderly couple were arguing about who should make the coffee in the morning. The wife said, "I think you should do it because you get up first." The husband countered his wife, saying, "The kitchen is your domain, and you do all the cooking, and you know where things are. I think you should make the coffee." "No way," she said, "You should do it. The Bible even says so." "What the heck are you talking about? Where does the Bible say that the husband should make coffee for his wife every morning?" the husband argued. His wife immediately grabbed the family Bible, thumbed through it, and pointed to the appropriate section which read: "Hebrews" (He-brews). Not competition and argument but loving care and generous support for each other will make family life meaningful and enjoyable. The Liturgy of the Word today presents Saint Joseph and the Virgin Mary as a pious and devout Jewish couple who formed their family to be God's holy temple. They faithfully observed the religious laws and customs regarding circumcision, purification, and presentation of the first-born (cf. Lk 2:22). Jesus the Messiah, as the consolation of Israel (v. 32), grew up in a family that was deeply immersed in the religious and social traditions of Israel.

Jesus' parents, in fact, represent the pious and expectant "people of God"; but at the same time, in their real lives, they also represent "the poor of

Yahweh." In accordance with the Mosaic Law in Leviticus (12:6), the mother is to offer a year-old lamb for her purification; but if she is poor, she can offer a pair of turtledoves or pigeons (v. 8). Since Joseph and Mary offered a pair of turtledoves (cf. Lk 2:23–24), they are thus portrayed as members of the poor of the land. The Holy Family indeed encountered severe hardships and challenges, trials and struggles, in fulfilling God's plan of salvation. Yet what affected their lives was not the poverty or problems of daily life, but rather their faith-conviction and trust in the promise of God, which strengthened and united them as one family. With the experience of God in their lives, Joseph and Mary created a healthy family atmosphere in which "The child [Jesus] grew and became strong, filled with wisdom; and the favor of God was upon him" (Lk 2:40). The experience of the Holy Family shows that the family that is grounded in God's love, with Jesus Christ at its head, will be united together in love, and dedicated to a common good. The Sage in the Book of Sirach assures us that in such families children are loved, parents are respected and honored, and above all, God is glorified (cf. Sir 3:1–11). The reason for many families who are falling apart in our society today is the absence of God in their life, and their failure to truly love one another. As Saint John Paul II has said, "The history of mankind, the history of salvation, passes by way of the family. The family is placed at the center of the great struggle between good and evil, between life and death, between love and all that is opposed to love." The noble virtues like compassion, kindness, meekness, patience, and forgiveness (cf. Col 3: 12-13) will adorn such families. Ask yourself: as a parent, do I create a loving family atmosphere so that all can grow in mutual love and wisdom, and in fear of the Lord? Do I experience the presence of Jesus in my family?

Wisdom from St. Francis de Sales: "You must do what you see can be done with love; there will be aversion and repugnance in your spirit, but we must do well and in a holy and loving way what we owe to everyone. Embrace holy prayer. Often throw your heart into the hands of God, rest your soul in His love, and put your cares under His protection. Do well what you can, and the rest leave to God who will do it sooner or later, according to the disposition of His divine providence" (SFS, *Thy Will Be Done,* 54).

Prayer: Lord God, thank You for giving us the Holy Family as an inspiration for our families. Bless my family, that we may grow in faith and love, and learn to live in happiness and peace.

The Solemnity of Mary, the Mother of God - January 1st

Num 6:22–27; Gal 4:4–7; Lk 2:16–21

Preparation: Take a few minutes of silence, setting aside all your worries and anxieties, and become aware of the divine presence.

Listening to God's Word: "All who heard it were amazed by what had been told them by the shepherds. And Mary kept all these things, reflecting on them in her heart. Then the shepherds returned, glorifying and praising God for all they had heard and seen, just as it had been told to them" (Lk 2:18–20).

A year of grace and hope

Once, a young man who was away from home wanted to call his parents on New Year's Day and wish them a happy new year. When he called, his Dad answered the phone. The young man said, "Happy New Year, Dad, and by the way, what's your New Year's resolution?" "To make your mother as happy as I can, all year," the father answered proudly. Then, greeting his mother, he asked her, "What's your resolution, Mom?" "To make sure that your Dad keeps his New Year's resolution at any cost," she replied. The experience of having something new will often be the happiest and most exciting moment in our lives. Now we are at the dawn of another new year, which reminds us that God still loves us, and that our lives have been gifted with another year. In the past year, we may have had both the happiest and the saddest experiences, both joyful and painful moments. All of these are important to make our life successful and happy in the New Year. Today the Liturgy of the Word presents us the model of two people, namely, that of our Mother Mary and of the shepherds. We are told that Mary treasured everything in her heart and pondered over it (Lk 2:19). In spite of the hardships, difficulties and struggles she encountered in her life due to her submission to God's Will, she experienced some wonderful things as well. Mary reflected upon all the awesome blessings of God. She realized that everything, even pain and suffering, had meaning for her. That is why she could discern God's will, and understand the meaning of her call to be the Mother of God.

Believing implies a faith-filled journey of searching for the meaning of each event in one's life. Mary was committed to following God's will in everyday happenings on her faith-journey and to paving the way for the redemption of the world. She approached life with optimism and with deep faith in the promise of God. This was her vision of life. We heard from the Gospel narrative that the shepherds went to Bethlehem, saw the Messiah, and proclaimed the Good News to others (cf. Lk 2:15–17). This was their mission. As disciples of Jesus, we are called to begin this New Year with the vision of Mary, trusting in God's promises of blessings, and continuing our mission to proclaim the message of salvation as the shepherds did. We need to be people of optimism and faith, surrendering to the Lord in everything with complete trust in His love. In all that may happen to us in this New Year, let us turn to God in child-like faith and cry out to Him, "Abba, Father!" (Gal 4:6). At the dawn of this New Year, let our prayer for each other be, "The Lord bless you and keep you! The Lord let his face shine upon you, and be gracious to you! The Lord look upon you kindly and give you peace!" (Num 6:24–26). By this prayer of blessing, the people of Israel experienced God's nearness and graciousness in their needs and trials. It also expresses God's continued protection and providential care in the everyday happenings of life. As pilgrims, we may experience ups and downs, and moments of light and darkness in our faith-life. Let the Virgin Mary's testimony of faith be a message of encouragement for us to move forward in optimism. Let us accept in gratitude all that may happen to us, and receive in faith and joy all that will be given to us in this New Year so that it will be a year of grace and hope. Ask yourself: do I cherish with gratitude all the wonderful ways in which God has intervened in my past life? How will I grow as a person of faith and optimism in this New Year?

Wisdom from St. Francis de Sales: "Desire nothing, refuse nothing. Look at the infant Jesus in the manger, who accepts poverty, nakedness, the company of animals and all the inclemencies of weather. At the same time, He experiences the warmth of love from His parents Mary and Joseph, the adoration of the wise men and of the shepherds, all with equal indifference. So, too, we ought to desire nothing and refuse nothing, but accept with perfect evenness of mind all that the providence of God may allow to happen to us" (SFS, *The Art of Loving God,* 142-143).

Prayer: Lord Jesus, thank You for the gift of this New Year. Guide me throughout this year to follow You in steadfast love and trust, making this New Year full of grace and hope.

The Epiphany of the Lord

Is 60:1–6; Eph 3:2–3, 5–6; Mt 2:1–12

Preparation: Take a few minutes of silence, setting aside all your worries and anxieties, and become aware of the divine presence.

Listening to God's Word: "They were overjoyed at seeing the star, and on entering the house they saw the child with Mary his mother. They prostrated themselves and did him homage. Then they opened their treasures and offered him gifts of gold, frankincense, and myrrh. And having been warned in a dream not to return to Herod, they departed for their country by another way" (Mt 2:10–12).

Salvation for all who seek

"No one is excluded; all are included. All those who seek with a sincere heart will experience the Lord's salvation." This is the central message of today's feast. There is an old Jewish legend: when the three Wise Men were following the star to Bethlehem, they came to the house of a certain woman. They said to her, "Come with us! We have seen His star in the East and we are going to worship Him, the Messiah." The woman responded, "Oh! I would love to come with you to see Him. I heard that He would be coming one day and I have been looking forward to that joyful day. But I cannot come now because I am too busy with my household work and have a few important appointments. So, let me finish all my work, and then I will follow you to find and worship Him." By the time she completed all her works, the Wise Men had disappeared. The star was no longer in the sky. She never saw the Messiah. The message is that it is difficult and challenging; yet, if we seek Him with a sincere heart and with perseverance, we will certainly find Him. In fact, the journey of the Wise Men is an image of our own faith-journey. In their search, they left behind all that belonged to them—their homeland, family, possessions—and journeyed to an unknown place. The way was unclear, the people were unfamiliar, and the fear of uncertainty and insecurity frightened them. These were the realities, the hurdles and obstacles, of their journey. Yet, they persevered in their search, and finally found the Messiah.

As believers, we are called to be seekers of truth, with perseverance, like the Wise Men. Many saw the star, but only the Wise Men grasped its message and followed it. They became seekers and pilgrims in their search. The result of their dangerous journey was that they experienced the light of salvation. The star has come to represent enlightenment. All those who encounter the Lord in life will be enlightened, renewed, consoled, and comforted. The Wise Men received not only enlightenment but also a new direction and purpose in life. So, they went back to their home country "by another way" (Mt 2:12). In a biblical sense "another way" could mean interior conversion and new direction. Thus, the Wise Men became missionaries, proclaiming the message of salvation. Ancient Israel believed, and the Church continues to believe and proclaim, that God's kindness is revealed to all, regardless of their race or ethnic origin. Therefore, Isaiah foretold, "Your light has come; the glory of the Lord shines upon you" (Is 60:1). Saint Paul the Apostle teaches that "the Gentiles [too] are coheirs, members of the same body, and copartners in the promise in Christ Jesus" (Eph 3:6). Hence, regardless of the number of the Wise Men or their cultural profile, the overarching message of this feast is the universal scope of God's salvation. Christ the Messiah has come as the light of the world. All are called to rejoice in the glory of the Lord. In our faith-life, while we are aware of the signs of God's dynamic presence that strengthens and motivates us in our faith-journey, we also must know of the obstacles that could hinder us from coming to the light. Ask yourself: like those Wise Men, do I follow Jesus the Light, to overcome the obstacles in my life? Do I learn to see the light of the Lord's salvation in moments of discouragements and despair, failures and problems?

Wisdom from St. Francis de Sales: "Persevere in overcoming yourself in the little everyday frustrations that bother you; let your best efforts be directed there. God wishes nothing else of you at present, so don't waste time doing anything else. Don't sow your desires in someone else's garden; just cultivate your own as best you can; don't long to be other than what you are, but desire to be thoroughly what you are. Direct your thoughts to being very good at that and to bearing the crosses, little or great, that you will find there" (Marie Thibert, *Letters of Spiritual Direction,* 112).

Prayer: Jesus my Savior, You are the Star of Hope for new life. Enable me to seek You in my life, and to overcome all hurdles and barriers, that I might experience the light of Your salvation.

Bibliography

Adams, James E. *Living Hope*. Fenton, MO: Creative Communications, 2007.

Camus, Jean Pierre. *The Spirit of St. Francis de Sales.* Champaign, IL: Book Jungle, 2008.

De Mello, Anthony. *Prayer of the Frog.* Gujarat, India: Gujarat Sahitya Prakash, 1989.

______________. *One Minute Wisdom.* New York, NY: Image Books, 1985.

______________. *Song of the Bird.* New York, NY: Image Books, 1982.

De Sales, St. Francis. *Introduction to the Devout Life,* Second Revised Edition. Bangalore, India: SFS Publications, 1995.

________________. *Thy Will Be Done: Letters to Persons in the World.* Manchester, NH: Sophia Institute Press, 1995.

________________. *Treatise on the Love of God,* Vol. 1. Bangalore, India: SFS Publications, 2009.

________________. *The Art of Loving God.* Manchester, NH: Sophia Institute Press, 1998.

Fiorelli, Lewis S., ed. *The Sermons of St. Francis de Sales on Our Lady.* Rockford, IL: Tan Books and Publishers, Inc., 1985.

Harrington, Daniel J. *Sacra Pagina: The Gospel of Matthew.* Collegeville, MN: The Liturgical Press, 1991.

Klauder, Francis J., ed. *Every Day with Saint Francis de Sales.* New Rochelle, NY: Salesiana Publishers, 1985.

Larsen, Earnie and Carole Hegarty. *Believing in Myself.* New York, NY: Simon and Schuster, A Fireside Book, 1991.

Mueller, Steve, ed. *God with Us.* St. Louis, MO: All Saints Press, 2013.

Thibert, Peronne Marie, trans. *Francis de Sales, Jane de Chantal: Letters of Spiritual Direction*. Mahwah, NY: Paulist Press, 1988.

__________________________. *Golden Counsels of Saint Francis de Sales.* Monastery of the Visitation, St. Louis, MO, 2006.

Tissot, Joseph. *The Art of Utilizing Our Faults According to St. Francis de Sales.* Bangalore, India: SFS Publications, Second Revised Edition, 1994.

Visitation, Nuns of the, trans. *The Sermons of St. Francis de Sales for Advent and Christmas.* Rockford, IL: Tan Books and Publishers, Inc., 1987.

I sincerely thank the Diocesan Publication, Grand Rapids, Michigan for the permission to use the Advent-Christmas clip art pictures.

Joy to the World is the latest in the Biblical spirituality series of Fr. Santhiyagu Arockiyasamy. This familiar title captures the angelic joy of the Advent event and the joy of those who enter into this holy season. Truly Advent (coming) is Joy! On fire with faith and zeal, Fr. Santhiyagu has devoted himself and his many gifts to bring a harmony of grace into this eye opener about Advent—the coming. Alive in the text is his pastoral sensitivity for the readers. He is a religious on fire in the charism of St. Francis de Sales. Faith and reason as well as divinity and humanity play their roles in Advent. The Son of God who becomes one of us (God with a face) is supremely Advent and so the Christian life is Advent as a way of life. The centerpiece is the reflection on the Gospel readings of the seasons of Advent and Christmas. Fr. Santhiyagu also quotes a host of profound spiritual insights from many fathers of the Church and great saints both past and present. Formed and guided by the Salesian charism and with confident devotion to St. Francis de Sales, Fr. Santhiyagu sums up each day with practical spiritual wisdom of this great saint of holiness.

Most Rev. Carl F. Mengeling
Bishop Emeritus
Lansing, Michigan

"What is the use of building castles in Spain if we have to live in France?" is an invitation from St. Francis de Sales to love what God loves. God loves our vocation, whatever it is, and so let us also love it here and now instead of thinking of the vocations of others. The wisdom of St. Francis de Sales urges us to let go of any anxiety which steals our inner joy that God desires for us. How do we find that joy? Fr. Santhiyagu Arockiyasamy, from his experience of prayer, parish ministry, and a spiritual journey in the steps of St. Francis de Sales, shares with us in detail how to defeat our disappointments of life. He shows us as well how to find joy and freedom as outlined by readings from the Advent and Christmas seasons and from St. Francis de Sales. I hope that *Joy to the World* will be a blessing to any reader who looks for the inner joy that God offers through His greatest gift to us in His Son, Jesus Christ.

Rev. Fr. Abraham Vettuvelil, msfs
Superior General
Rome, Italy

Fr. Santhiyagu Arockiyasamy has crafted a wonderful series of readings about the ancient liturgical seasons of Advent and Christmas. It is well worth your time to read and ponder these thoughtful reflections. He has taken the scriptural readings of the Advent-Christmas seasons, along with past and current Catholic thinkers, and woven them together into a very challenging presentation. He asks the readers many questions which will produce some soul-searching, so they may become enriched in their spiritual life during this holy season.

Msgr. Michael D. Murphy,
Diocese of Lansing, Michigan

"Have that mind in you which was in Christ Jesus," St. Paul teaches. These Advent and Christmas meditations by Fr. Santhiyagu Arockiyasamy, deeply rooted in Gospel truth, help us to do that. With the wisdom of St. Francis de Sales, vivid examples, and soul-searching questions, he invites us to think and act as Jesus in our daily work and lives. This invitation is especially relevant in our relations with others to experience the hope, peace, and joy that Jesus offers us in this season.

Msgr. Robert D. Lunsford
Diocese of Lansing, Michigan

About the Author

Rev. Dr. Santhiyagu Arockiyasamy, msfs, is a member of the Missionaries of St. Francis de Sales, known as the Fransalians. He has been working as a pastor in different parishes for more than eighteen years in India and in the United States. At present he is the pastor of St. Mary parish in Flint in the Diocese of Lansing, Michigan. The author holds a Master of Arts in Tamil language from Annamalai University, Tamil Nadu, India, as well as a Doctor of Ministry in Biblical spirituality from Barry University in Florida. He is committed to serve God's people in the missions, promoting the people-centered spirituality of Jesus and the optimistic spiritual wisdom of St. Francis de Sales.

In addition to *Joy to the World: Advent-Christmas Meditations with St. Francis de Sales*, the "Biblical Spirituality Series" includes *Gospel Meditations for Lent: Coming Home to the Father.*

About Leonine Publishers

Leonine Publishers LLC makes fine Catholic literature available to Catholics throughout the English-speaking world. Leonine Publishers offers an innovative "hybrid" approach to book publication that helps authors as well as readers. Please visit our web site at www.leoninepublishers.com to learn more about us. Browse our online bookstore to find more solid Catholic titles to uplift, challenge, and inspire.

Our patron and namesake is Pope Leo XIII, a prudent, yet uncompromising pope during the stormy years at the close of the 19th century. Please join us as we ask his intercession for our family of readers and authors.

Do you have a book inside you? Visit our web site today. Leonine Publishers accepts manuscripts from Catholic authors like you. If your book is selected for publication, you will have an active part in the production process. This book is an example of our growing selection of literature for the busy Catholic reader of the 21st century.

www.leoninepublishers.com

CPSIA information can be obtained at www.ICGtesting.com
Printed in the USA
BVOW05s1306101114

373795BV00001BC/1/P

9 781942 190042